Never ~~fear~~
Your Fire

Real stories, by real women that remind us to keep going, that you are not alone, lessons are blessings and to NEVER give up!

Jennifer Michelle Capella
Featuring 17 Women Warriors

Never Fear Your Fire

Publisher: Marissa F. Cohen

www.PublishWithMarissa.com

Publication Date: May 2023

©2023 by Jennifer Michelle Capella

All Rights Reserved

Printed in USA

ISBN 10:

Dedication

This book is dedicated to ALL my Women Warriors!

Women Warriors come in all forms. Each woman is a warrior in her own way.

We are driven, we are magnetic and powerful. We do not let obstacles or the things that have happened in our lives define us. We may fall down but we don't stay down-we rise. We have conversations based on growth and abundance and act from a place of love. We overcome adversity and limitations that were once put on us. We use the word 'No' unapologetically. We clap for our fellow Warriors and say their names in rooms of opportunity.

Thank you to each Warrior Author who shared a chapter from their lives. You are fierce and are leading by example. Warriors don't fear their fire, they become it!

Jennifer Capella

Xox JennMichelle

Acknowledgements

Thank You!

Thank you to all the Warrior Women Authors for trusting me with your stories and inspiring me to push forward with this project. You, ladies, are the epitome of what a warrior is. We were not joined by mistake; everything has its purpose and I am so grateful and honored to know each and every one of you.

To my Mom and sister, Brittany. I cannot thank you enough for coming through in the clutch for me when I needed it the most during this process. I am so lucky to have a mom and sister who I can count on no matter what.

To my Immediate Family- The Pollack's, Quigley's, Pasquin's, and McQuillian's.

This year has been one of the hardest in my life. One thing in life I know for certain I was blessed with was the family I was born into. Thank you for helping me with my girls. Doctors visit and/or my sanity at times. Thank you for always showing up and being there when it was needed the most.

To my husband, Jonathan. Thank you for always supporting me in whatever endeavor I decide to start. I am grateful for your love and for doing this life with me. I am so proud of the family we created. I love you endlessly.

To my beautiful daughters, Kailey, Jaianna, and Aleena. I can never thank God enough for you three. You girls have been my strength when I needed it the most with simply being yourselves. If I did one thing right- it's you girls. My forever friends, my pride and joy, and my heartbeats. Love you more than I can ever put into words.

To my baby boy- Jonathan Nathaniel. Thank you, my sweet boy. You have changed me into a better person. Because of you, I appreciate things more, I have more patience and I look at life differently. You have made our family stronger and better than ever. You have filled our home and my heart with so much happiness and love. I love your big smile, your eyes, and your spirit. You are the most beautiful baby, truly heaven-sent.

Table of Contents

Chapter 1:
1 in 700

Jenn Michelle Capella

We all have many chapters in our lives and when you put them all together they make us who we are-a Woman Warrior. Some chapters in our lives are our survival stories, some are our winning season chapters, some we may even want to forget, and then there are some that change us in ways that we never saw coming but we needed. Put all these chapters together and be proud of where you are at this very moment. Look at what you have overcome and accomplished, notice your mindset, and how unbelievably strong you are Warrior!

Life sometimes throws those curveballs. One thing I have learned is to take things day by day. I know that good or bad times do not last forever. There are so many things in life that are out of our control. However, how you handle those curveballs is what keeps you going. I truly do believe that God does not give you more than you can handle. Even though you say to yourself, "I know I'm strong but take it easy on me!' So this is my 1 in 700 Chapter. You are probably saying to yourself what's 1 in 700? No, I did not pick nusmbers and they were called, and now I'm a mega-millionaire. Even though that would be nice, that's not my story. My 1 in 700 has no dollar amount attached to it. I guess you can say I hit the lotto in another way- I was blessed with a beautiful baby boy and he is my 1 in 700.

Finally, I was at a great stage in my life. My three girls- Kailey, Jaianna, and Aleena were at the ages where they were becoming more independent and parent duties were not so tough. My beauty career was at a point where I was working with major television networks, I had consistent clients, and my beauty brand, Glamlife Beauty was finally taking off. I was seeing the fruits of my labor and was continuously growing. I started organizing women's networking events that consistently would sell out. I created Growth Group mornings and individual coaching that was sold out every month. Things were coming together and I couldn't ask for more. I was living in my prayers. I was in my winning chapter, on cloud nine. Everything I wanted to do was happening. I always believed that when you are in your winning season, you should help others along the way- and that's exactly what I did. My girls were all healthy, my husband and I were happy- it was only up from here! Then in January 2022, God decided to throw me a curve ball or so I thought this was it- I was pregnant with my fourth child.

When the pink lines appeared on my home pregnancy test, I ran out of the bathroom and told my husband. We smiled and were just overjoyed. We knew this was our last baby! Some people said I was crazy. I was almost 40, my life was set, and my girls were out of the baby stage. Some people even asked me if this was planned. To every person who planned their babies, kudos to you all. The reality is most children are not planned and I'm not mad about it. If you are here, you are a miracle anyway you look at it. Yes, my girls were out of the baby stage but now they can experience their youngest sibling and I was so happy for them. I am the oldest of four sisters and I remember when I was younger, how very proud I felt when my sisters were born. Now my girls can experience that. Now, I would be lying if I didn't admit that I did analyze from time to time if I was nuts to have a "geriatric pregnancy" as the doctors called it. (Yes geriatric! haha). Even though I was nervous when the reality of all the ways life would change again. However, the pros overpowered the cons by way too much to make me feel that this was nothing other than the missing piece to my family puzzle. I was ready to just enjoy every last ounce of my last pregnancy and couldn't have been any happier for this unexpected blessing.

I wanted to do all the mommy-to-be things because I knew this was my LAST time. The gender reveal party, the maternity shoots, the cravings (the best part if you ask me), the sonograms and just enjoying the preparation and anticipation of another addition that I would get to love with all my heart. My gender reveal was perfect! The weather was perfect, all our closest family and friends were there and the day landed on my husband's birthday weekend. As my mom handed us the smoke shooters, I felt butterflies, the time was here! Is it a boy or girl?! A part of me felt like this may be my boy but I already had three girls and I was a professional girl maker or so I thought. 1-2-3- POOF!! It's a boy!! The look of shock was all over my face! My husband, the girls and I started jumping up and down. Our friends and family were cheering- it was a perfect moment to end a perfect day. Even though it never mattered to us whether it was one more girl to love or a boy, to end the chapter in our lives of having babies with a boy- we couldn't have asked for more.

The following week was our long-awaited sonogram. My husband and I couldn't wait to see our boy. I also needed to verify with the tech one more time or two to make sure it was definitely a boy. I did this until I had the baby! Haha. During the sonogram, I noticed the tech took a little longer than usual. I was not too worried because I figured the baby is bigger now, and they are just taking measurements and

4

doing all the routine checks. After she was done, she told us she wanted to show the doctor and would be right back. Again, this was normal in the previous sonograms. About 15 minutes passed, and the doctor and the tech came back in. I instantly did not have a good feeling as the doctor started to do the ultrasound. The doctor looked for a few minutes and told my husband and me that they found something on the ultrasound that may affect the outcome of this pregnancy. "Your baby is going to be born with a cleft lip and palate and it's rather extravagant". I burst out in tears! I was uncontrollably crying, and as I reached out to my husband to hold his hand, I can tell he was crying too. As I lay sobbing, a million different things were running through my head. "Why me!?... My poor baby!.. Maybe she's wrong." I truly felt this was still not my reality because I don't even know anyone who has this! I was angry at the doctor and was in utter disbelief. Immediately after breaking the news to us, she went on to tell me that I may have to look into different options. Basically, she was telling me, I may not even be able to carry out this pregnancy because the quality of life would not be fair to bring this child into the world. Most babies born with clefts usually have some type of genetic condition, so I should be prepared for other options or "termination". She then went on to tell us about doing an amniocentesis. This is where they stick a long needle through your stomach to extract straight from the placenta. I agreed and the next month was the longest month of my life awaiting results. At this time, my stomach just popped and I felt my baby kicking. I was a wreck.

The next week, I did not want to do anything but cry. I was living in a nightmare or at least that is what it felt like to me. One thing about hard times, you feel like they can never happen to you, you are the only one experiencing it and you're never going to come out of it. One day my girls came home from school and they asked me what was going on with this baby. Kids are smarter than you think and are fully aware when something is off. I explained to them how the baby may be born. They basically looked at me and said, "So what Mom, he's our baby". They were right! So what! Maybe at the beginning of his life things would be a little different but God sent me this boy because he knew that if anyone would fight for someone they love it would be me! My girls are still young to not even realize how much strength they filled me with by simply being them. Blessed.

A month went by, all the results came back finally and everything was "normal". Thank God! During this time, all I did was google cleft lip and palates. I started to find groups on Facebook that other moms and families who had a Cleftie Warrior were a part of. I would read their stories, announcements, and before and after pictures of their beautiful babies. These groups helped me tremendously during this time and to this day. I found a community where I felt I was not alone in this new journey of motherhood and I did not feel judged either. I can ask questions and relate to the other expectant moms and was amazed by the moms who already had cleft baby warriors. I couldn't believe how many babies are born with cleft lips and palates. There was peace in knowing that I was not the only person going through this. I had hope. I knew the road ahead was not an easy one, but I was ready to make sure my baby was going to have all the things he needed. I am my child's advocate. If anyone is going to fight for him it is me. The first thing I did was I started educating myself on different ways of caring for my baby. During this process, I found CHOP, The Children's Hospital of Philadelphia. I could not have found a better place. I didn't care about the long drive, I needed to be in the best place because my son needed it. Most hospitals do not know how to feed cleft babies and I needed hands-on once he was born.

(Thank you to my Facebook group). The first day I went, it was a full day of testing. All tests came back good. The doctor told me he is a healthy baby boy, and they were not concerned whatsoever with his cleft lip or palate, they even gave me the measurement of the cleft. He had a team before he was born ready for his arrival. I knew we were in the best place. I decided to give birth there as well. The entire rest of my pregnancy was filled with happiness, joy, excitement, and all the things I was ready for once I found out I was pregnant.

On September 29th at 3:43 am my son was born. I had him by c-section. He was my easiest delivery. I remember when the doctors first saw him, they said "Wow, he has a full head of hair". They showed him through the plastic drape, I turned, looked at my husband, and said: "He's perfect". I was instantly in love and couldn't believe he was finally here. All my worrying was for nothing. For every mother who is reading this, I know you can relate as I write this with tears in my eyes thinking about the first time I laid eyes on my son, his first moments of life. There is nothing like seeing your child for the first time. Instant immense love.

A few hours later I was able to go see him and hold him for the first time. Ahh! My boy. I am a boy mom, I waited for this, I prayed for this. It was as if he knew it was me. The instant connection, my heart was so full and I was so in love. Dark hair, chubby cheeks, and big brown eyes- he was perfection. After only a week in the hospital, we got to take him home. We were so excited to bring him home and for his sisters to meet him. My husband and I couldn't wait to see them all together. Since he was born with a cleft lip and palate, we had to learn how to insert a feeding tube into his nose. Even though he ate from a bottle, it was important that he didn't burn calories. He had to maintain weight, so he needed a feeding tube after a half hour of feeding. Even though the transition was harder than with the girls I was up for it and was ready to give my son all that he needed to meet all requirements to not go back into the hospital. I cannot believe that I learned how to do a feeding tube. As mothers, we do whatever needs to be done for our children, and sometimes it's things we never can imagine doing. Don't get me wrong I cried every time because I did not want my baby to go through this but we did it because he needed it. After a while, my husband and I had a system and it was second nature. We still went to hospital visits weekly in CHOP and his regular pediatrician. When he was a few weeks old, he was given a NAM. It is a device that is somewhat of a retainer to help move his cleft closer together. The doctor insisted on him wearing the NAM 24 hours a day. I have never felt so defeated as a parent. He did not want anything to do with it. He would cry terribly, sometimes even cry it out. I felt terrible. I went back to my Facebook group and some moms did taping. I decided to tape his cheeks and mouth together in place of the NAM. His skin would be so irritated, under his nose, and by four months, he was so smart he figured out a way of opening it with his tongue. When we went back to CHOP to get his surgery date for his new smile, the doctor that was in charge of the NAM told me it was an act of love on my part to make him use the NAM. Really! I went on and told her all that I do is an act of love for this baby. Call it mother's intuition, but I knew in my heart my son was going to be okay. I was told to be prepared for him to just be on a feeding tube and in his first moments of life drink from a bottle. Yes, he needed to use one but not fully. I was told I may have to terminate this pregnancy because the quality of life may not be a livable one, I went by my faith and instincts and carried on and I gave birth to a healthy

8

baby boy. I felt deep down this was in God's hands, and he hasn't let me down yet. My son has beat the odds so far. Yes, his first years of life may be a little harder than most but he is here for a reason. He has already done so much in his first five months of life with just his presence. He is so special and one of the biggest blessings in my life and everyone that loves him. On March 24th, 2023 he will get his forever smile. He will have reconstructive surgery on his cleft and nose. Something while pregnant I couldn't wait for. I am filled with mixed emotions. He is my perfect boy. His big smile lights up the room and makes us so happy will forever change. I know all these things are necessities but it hurts my heart knowing the road ahead. When he is between nine months and one year old, he will have his palate surgery. At four years old, he will need bone graft surgery. They will remove bone from his hip and put it in his mouth and possibly reconstructive surgery if needed. He has weekly physical therapy and speech. One thing is for sure, I gave birth to a warrior. As much as I felt God gave him to me, he knew I would do anything and everything in my power to get him all he needs and just love him with every ounce of me. He was sent to me because I needed him. He has made me a better mother and a better person. I am more patient, kind, loving, open-minded, and more faithful. I've learned to surrender. The only way I can explain what it feels like to surrender is it's like an epiphany and it's powerful. I have never felt more like I am exactly where I am supposed to be. It's as if his life has put my life in perspective. I do not entertain things that don't feel good or get caught up in nonsense. I just want to be happy and live in gratitude and not waste any time. My family and house are happier. He made me stronger by giving me no choice but to step up and do what's needed. I am fearless. I am a Warrior Mom to a Warrior Son, my 1 in 700.

One in seven hundred babies are born with cleft lips and palates. These babies are resilient and strong little fighters. During this process, I have learned that you truly never know what someone is going through. Every baby is a blessing. To have a pregnancy without complications is rarer than ones with complications believe it or not. It is something that sometimes gets taken for granted. Listen to your intuition. Trust and believe that whatever you are going through, you are growing through and tap into the Warrior in you! Never fear your fire and know that you are capable of overcoming any situation thrown at you! Believe in yourself. Never give up and always show up as that Warrior Woman or Warrior Mom that you are!

Jonathan Nathaniel, 5-months

JennMichelle

TV/MediaCelebrity Makeup Artist + Hairstylist
Owner of GlamLife Beauty Collection
Founder of Women Warriors Collab
Cleft Warrior Mom
JennMichelle is CEO of **GlamLife** Beauty Collection, a Celebrity Makeup Artist & Hairstylist, Beauty Educator & Hair Extension Specialist, GlamLife TV Producer & Creator, Women's Empowerment Advocate, Entrepreneur and Cleft Lip and Palate Advocate.

She is currently the Makeup Artist and Hairstylist for The Lifestyle Today Show on CBS, Cover and feature hairstylist for Bella Magazine and NJ News. Founder of **GlamLifeBeauty Collection**, a product line of makeup and accessories for beauty professionals and makeup lovers worldwide. **Glam Life Beauty Collection** is a one stop shop for all your beauty needs.

With a long list of achievements, she has also worked New York Fashion Week, Miami Swimsuit Fashion Week, various movie and television sets including The Food Network, The Today Show, Chopped, Long Shot Production Company, Cool Magazine, Bridal Magazine, US Female Hockey Team, L'Oréal Events, QVC, For Women First Magazine, NBC, Good Housekeeping and more. She has also participated in photo shoots, off Broadway productions, and assisted with creating media content.

JennMichelle also founded **Women Warriors Collab**, a group of businesswomen who help to motivate, inspire, uplift, teach, and help one another through each level of their entrepreneurial journeys. They host meetings monthly to bring the group together as a collective and help to motivate, encourage, and teach one another different areas in business to help elevate each individual and brand. They also work together to give back to make a difference as much as possible

Lastly and most importantly, a mom of four. Three beautiful girls and a handsome little boy. A proud cleft warrior mom who is always here to show support and give hope to moms and families who are on the same journey as her.

You can follow her on Instagram **@jennmichelle_glamlife** **@womenwarriorscollab**

Chapter 2:
I'm Just a Girl from The Heights... That's Washington Heights to You...

Petronilla Gonzalez

When people ask where I'm from I will proudly tell you I'm from "the Heights" or Uptown. So, who am I? I am a simple girl from the neighborhood born into a first-generation Dominican family. I'm a daughter, mother, sister, caregiver, friend, multiple sexual assault survivor, multiple domestic violence survivor, sexual molestation survivor, bullying survivor, severe depression survivor, endometriosis survivor, two-time divorcée, empty nester, former NYPD Police Officer, former construction project manager and currently a happy small business owner. Yes, a survivor of all and master of healing from none. Every time I thought of how I would tell this story all that would come to mind was the sound of the Mr. Softee truck and the sensation of ice-cold water streaming out of the fire hydrants on a typical hot summer day in the Heights. A time in my life that was filled with pure love and innocence. The memory is always so cozy.

Growing up in Washington Heights was truly magical. Despite all the things, I grew up as a happy kid with a big heart and imagination. My babysitter Chela would call me "Petronila, the Famous One". She felt my creative imagination would lead me to big things one day. She was right but, little did I know that one day those dreams and innocence would be tainted with a darkness I was never prepared for. Somehow, when I finally encountered this darkness, I could always see a glimpse of light. The light that would give me hope and promise that one day things would be better.

I've learned that if you hold onto the darkness, you're never free. You become a prisoner of your past. You can never fully embrace the light if you keep the darkness in the shadow. I was raised with structure and very strong family values nevertheless, sometimes the things we are taught do not prevent or save us from bad situations or bad people. My neighborhood had a lot of good and genuine people. We did not see much of each other in the brutal Winter months but once the Spring rolled in The Heights would come alive. You would see everyone and everything. The energy of the neighborhood was just palpable. I loved those scorching summers in the 70's. Memories filled with polyester bell bottoms, tube tops, blaring boom boxes, playing hopscotch, sitting on the stoop, the fear of the Son of Sam, disco music and so on. I had a very loving, happy, and secure childhood. I loved all the things until life became as dark as the blackout of 1977. The first time I became a victim of sexual molestation. The first of many more incidents to come.

The traumas have been packed for a very long time and when I finally turned 50, I started thinking of how I could make this decade different. How could I make the other half of my life my best life and unpack all this shit I have been carrying. I decided it was time for a mid-life audit. Yes, I had to embrace the idea that it was time to do an external and internal life audit, especially feeling my 50's was starting to not look and feel the way I hoped. It was starting to depress me again. I must admit, just the thought of this process really scared me to the point of feeling emotionally paralyzed at times. I knew the internal purge had to start first and the picture was blurry, and I was feeling lost. My youngest daughter, Amanda,

17

told me that I needed to unfuck myself. My eldest daughter, Sue, was not happy I wasn't living my best life. I could not for the life of me figure out how to take the next steps. How to get unstuck and unfucked. It came down to the harsh reality that I needed to expose myself to myself so I can become the change I wanted to see. Although I have a strong sense of self-awareness, I was not being completely honest with myself. I was sugar coating my own shit and downplaying my reality.

The 50's are a tricky decade. You can either be where you want to be or at a crossroads. I think something shifts inside us as women at this point. It can be a good shift but also dangerous at the same time. You can wake up one day and realize you don't want to live the life you've always known. Nothing makes sense, you feel you have no purpose, no direction, or no growth. You can feel you've wasted years on senseless things and have nothing to show for it. You spend so many years looking after others that you overlook the most important part which is yourself. You have become depleted from years of pouring into others, yet your own cup is running on empty with no refills. Rarely does anyone pour into your cup. Life becomes a vicious cycle of constantly giving and running on fumes. In some instances when you finally decide to take care of yourself now all of a sudden, you're deemed as being selfish.

Then people wonder why is it that when we turn 50, we are so fucking tired. Well guess what? It is just not menopause that makes us tired, fat and maybe even a little crazy, it is literally everything we have lived and survived. I can really go in deep and talk about all the trauma but for now I will unpack one at a time. Right now, at this moment I feel I need to speak to my 50's club that are going through this crazy midlife transition while trying to heal from severe past traumas. Three years in so far, I think I am finally figuring out the path to pivoting and making this other half of life the best it can be. This is a new journey for me, and I am not rushing through it and most definitely will not feel bad about it. I talked to a lot of women and heard so many different experiences and stories about their own life transitions. Some want more peace, some want growth, some want Botox and tummy tucks, while others want to have extramarital affairs to spice things up, there are others that simply want NOTHING. This is a beautiful chapter for me despite so many messy things but as you get to know me the layers of 53 years will unravel, and I want to share what it has taught me.

Being molested at the tender age of six was something I thought I could ignore because I did not know how to speak of it. I was embarrassed and I did not want a pity party.

It started when I would go on my father's beer runs between the ages of six to seven. I enjoyed going to the store for him. It made me feel important and so grown up. I used to go to our neighborhood bodega up the block, but he decided after a while to send me to the one across the street as he could keep an eye out for me as I crossed the street back to our building. Little did my poor father know that the danger wasn't out in the street but rather inside that bodega that he would send me to.

There was this older, heavy-set man that hung out there every weekend. He was a friend of the bodega owner. He would always say hi to me when I entered the store, so I thought he was friendly. One day that all changed when he followed me to the back of the bodega where the beer refrigerators were located. He used the pretext of helping me find the beer brand I was looking for, but this was an excuse only to take advantage of me. He would lean into me from behind me and fondle me in a way I couldn't understand. I was only six at the time. I couldn't understand something of this magnitude when my focus was watching cartoons, playing with dolls and practicing my penmanship. That's what a six-year-olds life was like back then.

Every single fucking time I went to the store on the weekends he was there. I do not remember his face anymore, but till this day the stench of beer sometimes reminds me of him. I felt it was my fault and I allowed him to touch me because I didn't know how to defend myself. I started to talk to myself, acting out all the things I would say to him next time he touched me.

Now, I wonder what kind of sick bastard would want to fondle a six-year-old with undeveloped body parts. Probably the most developed part of me was my brain as I had a crazy obsession with reading the dictionary. I wasn't even going through puberty for Christ sakes.

After a while, I just learned to accept it and allow it as I didn't have the strength to fight it. The one thing I knew I could never do was tell my father. I knew that my father would have taken matters into his own hands and the last thing I wanted was for my father to go to prison. I think that would have been more painful than the abuse itself. Even to think of it now makes me sick. I could not fathom the idea of my father, the most hardworking and loving soul in my life, my best friend, wearing an orange jumpsuit paying for someone else's mistake.

At one point, I just told him I didn't want to go on anymore beer runs, and I never went back again but the feeling of being violated was something I couldn't shake off. I wish I had stopped the beer runs sooner but I didn't want to disappoint my dad. I wanted to run away and many times I attempted to, but I didn't get far. I would pack a shopping bag with clothes and go to my neighbor's house on the first floor. After a couple of hours, I would just go back home because I missed my parents. Everyone thought it was cute, but I knew what I was running away from.

I used to get bullied in school too and after a while a switch inside me just flipped. I was tired of being and feeling abused, I was so fucking over it. I started having fights in class, all the time, every week. My father could always expect a weekly call from Mr. Gross, the Principal, that I got into a fight AGAIN. I was either picking a fight or if another kid said something I didn't like, I flew into a state of rage. In one instance I hit one of the boys with my trumpet because he made fun of my dad. He was so terrified he accidentally ran into the girl's bathroom. No one could understand what I was going through or my behavior. Heck, I couldn't understand it myself. I couldn't bear to tell anyone that someone inappropriately touched my breasts and vagina without feeling shame or dirty. There was so much displaced anger, and my behavior grew increasingly bizarre. I think everyone started to chalk it up to my strong character. I wanted to take out my aggressions on my molester and I couldn't because I would never see him again. It was too late, and I was very angry about it.

Eventually, my father got the call that if I got into one more fight I would be suspended. Then it stopped. I didn't want to disappoint my dad. Now that I couldn't physically hit anyone, I started to verbally abuse other kids. After one of those verbally abusive engagements, I made one of my classmates so upset he threatened to kick my ass after school. As soon as that bell rang, he proceeded to swiftly kick me right in my ass and it hurt. After the initial shock, I swung around and grabbed my best friend's umbrella, and I swung it right in his face and caught him good in the eye. He ran home crying and his eye was black, blue, and swollen. Fuck, I had to tell my parents again that I got into another fight. My only saving grace was that this kid hit me first but the fact that I hit him with an umbrella and caused serious injury didn't go over well with my parents nor the principal.

I graduated from elementary school with very good grades nonetheless, but my next stop was Catholic school. There was zero tolerance for fighting and I knew I could not push any buttons because our principal, Sister Eileen, was not the one. I was verbally mean to other kids from time to time until I got in trouble for that as well and had to shut it down. The behavior went from there to boarding school and so on. I was mostly nice, funny, and entertaining but if someone said one thing that triggered me, it would set me off. I realize now the trauma had always been there because this behavior remained consistent throughout most of my life. I learned to cope and immerse myself in whatever I was doing at the time to keep so busy I wouldn't have time to think. I thought I forgot about it, or so I thought UNTIL that one day I had to pick up my ex-husband from work and he had to work overtime due to a case that came up with two very young girls that were victims of their father. It didn't add up right away. I thought maybe they were spanked, and their father went a little too far with the punishment. So naturally I asked what happened. I wasn't ready for it. Their father forced them to touch and fondle him while he masturbated in front of them. He wanted them to watch. He wanted them to watch him ejaculate and kiss and caress his penis. They clearly articulated his actions until the white stuff came out. He made them promise not to ever tell their mother because it was a special little secret between them. The mother didn't have an idea and eventually

22

found out when one of the girls told her she had a secret. The little girl wasn't even mad at her father, but she didn't want to participate in his depraved sex game any longer. It became a regular after school activity when he picked them up and they were tired of it. My ex-husband and partner asked me to go down to child services on Laight Street as the girls needed to stay there until the father was arraigned, the mother was interviewed, and the detectives could figure out how to proceed with the case. I sat in the back of the patrol car with the little girls during the transport and they were so animated still in their school uniforms asking where we were going not realizing what was about to happen. I was trying not to throw up. I hated dropping kids off at Laight Street. You never knew if the parents would get them back or if they would go into the foster system. Between that and child removals from the home I couldn't tell you, which was worse, but you must do the job. It can fuck you up a little in the head. You find coping mechanisms whether it's drinking, working excessive overtime, or making insensitive jokes. You must, it's a lot to carry. I was hoping they wouldn't replay the story and tell me what their father did to them. I had learned to cope and manage my tantrums somehow and once again I was sitting there triggered again. Those triggers were beginning to feel like an old friend passing through every now and then to say hi. I thought I shoved all the triggers and trauma in the closet, and they would never return again.

I thought I would never experience any type of sexual trauma again until the rapes, in plural, there was more than one. I think I have told a total of five people about it until now and three of those people used it against me. Imagine confiding in a partner that you had been sexually assaulted and during an argument they tell you that "you deserved to be raped". Clearly, I was engaging in relationships with the wrong people. I am not ready for that conversation yet. It doesn't hurt anymore but at this moment I don't care to replay those events. I did it this one time for one person, who needed to hear my story because she was a rape victim herself. I was still a Police Officer and one late night in Midtown towards the latter part of my tour we got a call of a robbery in progress on the east side of 42nd street. A lot of times they were bullshit calls, but you still approach with caution because the last thing you want is to walk into a robbery in progress blindly. My partner and I were not the first on the scene but eventually we were called over once the first unit confirmed it was indeed a robbery and requested a female police officer on the scene. I found it kind of odd, but you just go where you are needed, no questions asked. Well, not only did we walk into a past robbery but also a rape. Holy fuck! I had not heard the word "rape" in a long time but there we were. A male victim on his knees tied and robbed at gunpoint and a female victim raped at gunpoint and the male victim was forced to watch. They were both visibly shaken and the security officer for the building was nowhere to be found. We arrived to assess and clean up the mess. Obviously, we had a female sexual assault victim, and I was tasked to speak to her, console her, accompany her to the hospital and witness the Doctor perform the testing for the sex evidence collection kit. Ughhhhhh, talk about walking down memory lane in person. I wanted to say NO and I couldn't. I didn't want to help as awful as it sounds. I felt she was lucky because the police showed up to help and we were getting her medical assistance. I couldn't tell her she was lucky while she was still on her knees with a sore vagina. I never called the police, there were no evidence collection kits, there was no consolation, no hugs, no support, no one to call, no one to say everything would be okay. I wasn't as brave as she was, and it bothered me. I only had tears, disgust, and shame. How out of all the females in my command this had to happen on the 4x12 tour when I was the ONLY female???? I felt life was playing a very cruel joke on me. Rubbing the memories in my face and I felt like I had been suckered punched. We hung out in the emergency room at Bellevue Hospital, which was a complete shit show and chaos. A typical night in a city hospital emergency room. She kept asking if she could have a private room, she felt exposed although she was fully clothed. I knew that sinking feeling, feeling naked when you're not. I requested a room only to be told she needed to wait. Okay, we wait. Now she needs to use the bathroom which is a huge no-no. There is no peeing whatsoever when you have been sexually assaulted as they don't want the evidence to be flushed down the toilet. Like whom the fuck wants to keep the evidence inside of them anyways. I found a nurse and told her I needed the evidence collection process sped up because the victim needed to pee. This nasty nurse said the victim needed to wait because they were BUSY. Well, no shit, it is always busy. It took every bit of strength and composure not to lose my shit on this woman so I proceeded to say as my voice got louder, "if you were the one that was just raped would you be okay waiting". There was silence and a bit of shock, and I demanded a private room for the victim, or I was going to allow her to pee. Yes, we got the room quickly and now it was just the two of us, alone. Two rape victims silently sitting in a room just waiting. She was in a daze, and I was trying to curb the feelings of nausea and anxiety as once again I was triggered. She finally said something. She asked me how this could happen to her when all she was doing was cleaning offices because she needed a job to support her son. I am not going to lie, writing this right now is making me choke up. I remember the feelings clearly. A pretty and petite female, Hispanic, who migrated from Colombia for a better life and there she was laying on a hospital gurney, emotionally and mentally vulnerable, partially naked, and afraid. This was not the better life America was supposed to offer her. My heart just felt heavy and I kind of chuckled. A nervous chuckle. For a minute I didn't know what I could say.

Fuck, fuck, fuck...I had to or at least felt like I was forced to tell my story. I proceeded to tell her that I understood, and she looked at me completely confused. I had to tell her, that I too was raped. Not once, not twice but three times if statutory rape counts as one of them. I had to tell her I knew the feeling of just wanting to take a long hot shower hoping it would wash away the smell of sex, the semen, the saliva, the breath, the dirt left behind which no matter how hard you scrubbed you could not wash away. I remember going to my after-school job at Wendy's and putting on a big smile and pretending I was okay. I just wanted to run away again. She looked at me in disbelief. Here I was, this cute, twenty-five-year-old, 5'4", Hispanic, female Police Officer and a multiple rape victim. I heard the sigh of relief. I didn't give her any explicit details, but I told her I knew what she felt, and she was brave for calling for help. I had to tell her I never called for help, I never told anyone, I never did ANYTHING, I wasn't brave. I did absolutely nothing but hide it. She asked me what was next, and I told her we have to wait for the Doctor to perform the evidence collection kit and she was terrified. There she was getting ready to feel violated by another man, but I promised I would be there, holding her hand while he performed the test. I would make sure I watched EVERYTHING and assured her he wouldn't touch her inappropriately. I stood there and watched the swabbing, the extraction of pubic hairs one by one, and so forth. What a sinking feeling in the pit of my stomach. I wanted to run and there was nowhere to go. I was there until the next female officer from the midnight tour would come to relieve me and I can assure you she didn't show up at midnight, none of it her fault as her shift had less officers working so at that time getting to the hospital wasn't a priority. All I can say is when she finally arrived at one in the morning, I couldn't run out of Bellevue Hospital fast enough. I felt the pressure in my chest and the need for air, but I rushed back to my command, changed out of uniform, got in my car as quickly as I could to get back to my home in the Hudson Valley at the time. That was the beauty of living far from the city. I wasn't at risk of bumping into any of my former violators if you want to call them that or any perpetrators I may have arrested. Far removed from the noise, pollution, hustle, and bustle of the Boroughs. I felt safe in the Hudson Valley, and I liked it that way. My kids were safe too and that's all that mattered. That was the last time I have ever said the words "I was raped". Now I am saying it again but this time I am not ashamed, I am not disgusted, I am not embarrassed and most importantly, I am not afraid. I am not even ashamed of the domestic violence I lived through because now I understand it. I understand what happened, I know it was not my fault and I didn't deserve it. Just because something bad happens to us doesn't mean we deserved it or asked for it. It happened, period, end of story. Domestic violence is something I will share in the future. I am not mad about it anymore. I hold no ill feelings towards my aggressors. I have learned that broken people break other people, hurt people hurt other people and the cycle goes on. Two unhealed souls will eventually either heal together in a safe way or hurt each other even more. Sometimes we don't have the luxury to wait for someone to heal and sometimes they can't wait for us. Knowing what I know now, the unhealthiest of relationships is when two people are trying to fix or change the other. There is no fixing or changing, that's an individual journey that only you can do on your own. Healing is a very personal process. I don't know if I am completely healed, but I feel free. All the skeletons knocking on that closet door couldn't wait to come out. I can walk past the bodega today and not feel triggered anymore. I feel free and it brings happy tears although there are still so many things I am still working on. I am okay now working through them, I finally got out of my own way. I started the journey of unfucking myself. I owe so much to my daughters because they kept me going and loved me during so many years when I was unlovable and damaged. They always loved me despite the mess and the ugly times. I know this affected them and they have been on their own healing journey. They didn't ask for this, but they still loved me unconditionally and would wipe away my tears after every mistake and every failure. They were always my biggest cheerleaders right alongside my mother who supported me every way she could more so after my father passed away in 2000. They were my rock and didn't even know it. I continued to push through and tried to work hard to make my three biggest cheerleaders proud of me. My relationship with my daughters is different than most. It's not for anyone to understand but us. My mother on the other hand is non-verbal and paralyzed due to a massive stroke and although it's been literally six years since she suffered the initial stroke I feel like I have lost her. She is here in body but the mother I once knew is gone. The stroke robbed me of that. That still hurts a lot. There aren't any more daily check-in phone calls, no funny gossiping rants, no home cooked Spanish meals, no holidays, no warm motherly hugs, or I love you's. I will continue my healing journey and be the best version of myself. I owe it to her, my father and my two daughters. Life has beat me up quite a bit, but

I am still standing, and I feel blessed. I know firsthand it can always be worse. I have seen it many times. I have seen things most people have not nor will ever see. I am very excited for what the future holds and all the things that are yet to come. I'm excited to continue to work with my mentors, who in such a short time ignited the courage in me to tell my story. My work is not done, I have a lot to share, a lot to give, so many chapters of many more things but for now I just want to revel in this feeling. As Brooke Shields would say "the beginning is now". I am looking forward to this new beginning because now I am finally free.

To be continued....

Pat Gonzalez was born and raised in the upper sector of Manhattan also known as Washington Heights.

She comes from a first generation of Dominican immigrant parents and is profoundly proud of her roots.

Although American born, she considers herself as full Dominican. As a child, she was very passionate about all that life could offer and had a strong desire to excel in her future endeavors. She would be the first to tell you that her tenacity, perseverance, and fierce determination stem from values instilled by her parents. She hoped to make them proud as she witnessed the sacrifices and challenges her parents faced to provide a better life for her family.

A survivor of child molestation, sexual assault, multiple domestic violence incidents, and severe depression, she embarked on a personal development journey at the age of fifty-two to help her heal from years of buried traumas. Formerly a New York City Police Officer and Construction Project Manager, she holds two degrees from the notable Pratt Institute in New York. Recently, she made the

decision to close the chapter on her construction management career to oversee her mother's care.

During this time, she started her own Notary Signing Agent business where she conducts mortgage loan closings throughout the state of New Jersey.

Pat is the mother of two very successful adult daughters whom she is very proud of. As a single mother, raising two daughters while processing so much internal trauma was one of the most difficult experiences in her life. She has a fifteen-year-old Chihuahua which she considers a third daughter and credits for bringing joy and peace into her life throughout various hardships.

In her free time, she enjoys spending time with her daughters, weekends at her country home with her boyfriend, the beach, reading, watching renovation shows, networking and listening to music while she on the road.

Her dream is to continue scaling her business, explore new places, help other victims of sexual and domestic assault, and lastly, have the financial means to one day help and give to others just as her parents did.

This chapter is dedicated to my parents, Venecia and Jose Manuel, who gave me the tools to succeed in life but most importantly gave me so much love. I owe my hard work and dedication to them for all the endless sacrifices they made. I want to thank my beautiful daughters, Sue and Amanda for being my best friends and showing me the true meaning of unconditional love for another human being. Thank you for always holding my hand, making me laugh, and being there for me through the worst and best of everything. My sister Milly, and brother Joey, no matter the differences, you always show up for me and the love is always there. I also want to thank my boyfriend, Michael, for teaching me patience, deep love, and acceptance in this roller coaster we call life. Lastly, I want to thank Jennifer Capella and Nastasya Rose for their support, love, and mentorship, and for giving me the safe space I had been seeking all my life, there really aren't words to express my gratitude.

Chapter 3:
Celebrate Your Failures

Renee Marshall-McKinley

Founder of KYSS – Keep Yourself Smelling Sweet
www. MYKYSS.com

F ailures can look and feel differently for every individual. The dictionary defines failure as:

1. lack of success,
2. the omission of expected or required action.

Ellen DeGeneres once said, "It's failure that gives you the proper perspective on success."

What I know is that as an entrepreneur we can read too much into failure and tie it to our sense of self-worth, self-esteem, and self-acceptance. We must look at failures entirely differently. It is time to embrace and celebrate our failures!

Social media would have you believe that anything and everything an entrepreneur attempts went exactly as planned and everything it glitz, glam and glory. That is simply not the case for most of us entrepreneurs. You have seen them, the constant daily pictures and posts of entrepreneurs sporting the biggest smiles with the happiest eyes, poses from happy locations looking like a million bucks. Often, it is not real. These posts are to cover up the many times we have failed to succeed at one thing or another.

If you were to take those types of pictures at face value and not have a conversation with them, you would not know that they probably suffered failure more often than you would possibly think. Probably right before taking those happy pictures that were shared on their social media platforms, they failed at something that very day.

Six (6) Reasons to Celebrate Failures

1. Learn the Lessons In Failures

Failure teaches us what we do and do not want as we move ahead in business or in our personal lives. We must be open to learning the lesson that has been presented before us. We should often ask ourselves what this failure showed me. What is the lesson in this? Did I really make one mistake or several mistakes to get here?

We should sit and chat with ourselves to learn what could have changed so as to not fail the same way. What should I have done differently, what should I do next time to not repeat the same mistake ultimately leading to my failure?

Let me help you to understand a big lesson of failure. When you can bounce back from a failure or multiple failures it can teach your resilience. It has the capability to show you who you really are. You are stronger than you ever imagined you are. It is THAT quality that makes you show up and NOT quit on yourself. Resilience is the stuff that successful entrepreneurs will tell you that they are made of!

Do The Work:

List 6 lessons that you have learned from a recent failure:

1. _____

2. _____

3. _____

4. _____

5. _____

6. _____

2. Know That Failure Helps To Overcome Fear

Fear of failing can be paralyzing. Fear of failing can make you procrastinate; it can make you pause your life. As an entrepreneur you do not want to show your failures to your peers or customers. Failing is a scary position when it does happen. We fear failing because we do not want to be judged by others. It is not a great feeling when someone knows that you have failed, especially if it is publicly known. That is why entrepreneurs will share their successes publicly. It is

the feeling of acceptance that we want to hold on to. Who wants to be rejected? Rejection can feel like the biggest failure of them all.

Operating in a space to avoid failure can limit your ability to be successful. It can be very scary and lonely to face your fears. I know it does not sound like sound advice; but facing our fears may reduce the stress and discomfort we internalize by stepping or working out of our comfort zone.

Sometimes we must do the very thing or things that we are fearful of to move on to bigger and better things. This is where the learning takes place. Try new things in your business often, fail quickly, pick yourself up, try something different until you find that sweet spot. To be transparent, no one knows if you have failed. The good thing about it is that only you and God will know about your failures unless you are sharing your failures with the world. Even in the sharing it can be cathartic for you and helpful to someone else.

If you try and fail often, over time you may not have a BIG pit in your stomach, only a tiny pit. That is progress and you are learning from your failures. Celebrate the small wins no matter how frequent or infrequent they show up in your business.

Practice this acronym for **FEAR**:

Face Everything And RISE! Do The Work:

List 6 way that failure has helped you overcome fear:

1. _____

2. _____

3. _____

4. _____

5. _____

6. _____

3. Use Failure To Recommit To Goals

Failures can be extremely valuable. In failure, the opportunity to know yourself even better than you did when you were not failing or did not recognize that you were failing. It is here where you can really sit with yourself and reflect, recall, rethink and reconsider the failure in private. This is where you would consider if the failure were simply a mistake and not the end of everything like your business, your company brand, or your confidence in yourself.

It is this space where you begin to reevaluate, plan, and prepare better. Failures should help lead to the road of making better outcomes and goals sooner rather than later. Take this time to find new and better ways to strengthen, strategize and achieve new or refine goals. A good review and restructuring will lead to better and more refined goals.

Do The Work:

List 6 ways that failure has helped you to recommit to your goals:

1. _____

2. _____

3. _____

4. _____

5. _____

6. _____

4. Failure Inspires Creative Solutions

Coming up with a new idea is so wonderful. The internal brainstorming that can produce a new idea is also wonderful and powerful. Taking time to dream, wonder or be inspired by something or someone for the next creative idea is freaking awesome and yes, so scary too.

This is where you either find confidence or second guess yourself. Will people like what I have produced, or will they reject it and feel like a failure? We had all had this type of experience before, right? It is going to be the next biggest and boldest idea that you have ever had, you are so excited to show it until it's actually time to show it and then you are too frightened to introduce it to your customers. No one likes to be rejected but it is the fear of failure that has you second guessing yourself.

When you think that your idea was not good enough or you are not good enough – you know the negative self-speak that we do to ourselves all too often and for no reason. It will stifle you and your creative flow. But when you step back and allow yourself to feel your feelings and move on from them, that is where the magic happens. Often, we are not frightened so much by the idea itself, but by the reaction of others. Maybe we are also a bit fearful of being successful too.

Remember that without fear and without failure, there is no creativity and no possibility of success. Failing allows creativity to flow, to generate new ideas which can lead to even more success, even bigger than the previous creative idea that was thought of.

Do The Work:

List 6 ways that failure has inspired you to develop creative solutions:

1. _____

2. _____

3. _____

4. _____

5. _____

6. _____

5. Strengthens Your Support System Through Failure

We all fail. Period. At some point in our lives, yes, we have failed at something and that is OK. It is a part of life, and it is necessary to learn, grow and hopefully we become humble and kinder humans along the way. When we fail, it may be an extremely low part in our life or entrepreneurial journey or at least we feel like it is. There is nothing more necessary than to have

supportive relationships, such as knowing people who can provide you with information, advice, guidance, and tangible support, such as assistance in times of uncertainty. If we could, we would carry our childhood security blanket to wrap around us and to comfort us when we needed, but let's face it that's not adulting is it? Having tight social support can be comforting and enhance your feelings of security.

Supportive relationships can also pick you up and carry you emotionally when you are feeling down or overwhelmed. Our family, friends and trusted clergy, advisors or mentors will listen to our fears, hopes, and dreams, and make us feel seen, heard, and understood. They can help you think through alternatives from a different perspective and aid in solving problems, and they can distract you from your worries, fears and doubts when that is what is really needed. In doing all this they provide encouragement and lower your stress and feelings of loneliness when facing failures. There is power in numbers and connections. Appreciate your circle, rely on them and carry on.

Do The Work:

List 6 ways that failure has strengthened your support system:

1. _____

2. _____

3. _____

4. _____

5. _____

6. _____

6. Failures Make A Great Story

Who does NOT love the underdog? It is in the failures that can make us a more interesting person and entrepreneur. It is the struggle that holds all the character-building gems, it is the struggle that makes us truly appreciate what we have built and reminds us of our humble beginnings. It also keeps our ego in check.

Let's face it, most of us, the small entrepreneurs have to work ten times harder, talk to 100 more people, start up with far less capital and usually doing all of this as a solopreneur while working a fulltime job, responsible for the household and declining time to spend with our family and friends just to stay even or barely above water.

Failures can make us more relatable, and seem more real to others. You know, and I am sure you have heard it before... If I can do it, so can you! And that is the truth of the story. People may admire you more when things did not go as planned or if you failed often but were able to pick yourself back up to be successful.

Failures can make you hungry for success. Failures can motivate you to work all night, be focused and may motivate the people in your circle to support you more. There is admiration of others when they know the intimate details of the rags to riches, failure to success stories. Share your story often; you may just inspire the next entrepreneur.

Do The Work:

List 6 way that failure may make your story great:

1. _____

2. _____

3. _____

4. _____

5. _____

6. _____

Failure does hurt, may even cause you to pause, and have an impact on your ability to be a happy, successful, and fulfilled entrepreneur. As I stated earlier, fail and do it often. Things really will be OK. Find the lessons that are there, you may need to dig a bit deeper to see and understand them, but they are truly there for your growth and guides us toward needed improvement for a more successful future. Embrace and celebrate the failures, they are important to success!

 Renee Marshall-McKinley is the award-winning CEO and Founder of Keep Yourself Smelling Sweet – KYSS®. She started her entrepreneurial journey in 2012 by providing a line of natural bath, body, and hair care products that promote a healthy, sweet-smelling cleanliness without breaking the bank.

She makes time to give back to her community by giving of her time and talents to several major and local non-profit organizations. KYSS donates money, goods and services to not-for-profit organizations on a local and national level.

Renee is a philanthropist and speaker who facilitates workshops across the US to encourage confidence and inspire others to learn to make and or start their own beauty care or candle business.

As a result of her service to the community, she has received awards to include Project Re-Direct Business and Community Service Award, Odyssey IP Business Award and more. She was selected by Essence Magazine as one of the Top 50 Founders to Watch and received a personalized Thank You from former First Lady, Michelle Obama.

Renee and her daughter, Jocelyn, joined forces in October 2020 to launch their first joint venture, Belles In Bloom® A Pictorial Experience as another opportunity to promote and encourage girls and women of all ages to love themselves and the women they may meet.

Dear God,

Thank you for the drive and perseverance to never give up on myself. Period!

To my parents, Howard and Joyce for teaching me that failing is not failing at all when you get up and try again. Thank you for teaching me failures are where the learning takes place! I'm so grateful!

To my family for accepting me during my failures and loving me anyway. I could not do any of this without YOU!

My love always,

Renee

Best,
Renee Marshall-McKinley
Http://BellesInBloom.com

Chapter 4:
She is All in One

Christina Fernandez

W ho is she?
She is the creator of the idea that only some supported

The boss of the side job that was building an empire

The true Hustler that always had 2 jobs

The artist that worked hard to master her skill

The hopeless dreamer that was told to go back to her 9-5

She is the creator of the mastermind behind the brand

She is a risk taker of something meant to stand

A educator sharing what she knows

Enduring everything that tried to break her

She is the artist that very few came to support

They encouraged her to abandon ship, mission abort

She is the beauty and the brains

The one holding the reigns

Who is SHE?

SHE IS me.

SHE IS **All In One Beauti.**

Beauty knows no bounds

Walk in, you're welcomed with a smile

A five star beauty business taking over **BK**

Servicing clients with good taste

What hard work it takes

Working 23 hours or 12-hour days

Late night clients just to get paid

Very few friends, limited days and misunderstood

Being her own cheerleader when the texts end up dead

A part time makeup artist starting at just 18

She turned her hustle into a dream

You only do great work when you love what you do

What a difference this life makes when work is fun for you!

There is nothing she won't do,

And at times, overworked.

Behind that woman there's a little girl

Behind that girl, there is a life without a Mother

How fast it all got taken away

Falling to her tragic death, shocked them all

Having just given birth,

The perfect family was at a loss.

Where will she live?

Where will she go?

Who would take that baby girl at just two months old?

She will stay here, in this very place

Where her Mommy left her so Grandma can take her place

As she waits in heaven, watching with no control

Everywhere she goes -

Holding her hand when she falls

Wiping her tears when she fears

Who she prayed for, who she created, who she left behind

Someone so small!

How painful, how frustrating!

To watch and do nothing at all

Can you imagine watching down from heaven at your baby girl?

How can this happen? Why me? Can I come back?

I can't leave her so small

Who will hold her hand on her first day of school?

Don't be scared baby, I haven't left.

I'm still here.

Raised by Grandma until four years old

What wonderful, fulfilling years!

Daddy made a call,

"I'm married. I'm moving. Can I take her home?"

Leaving Grandma's, as clear as day

Holding onto the banister, kicking and screaming

PLEASE don't take me away!

If she only held tighter, would Daddy have let her stay?

If only Grandma had fought harder to keep her close,

She might have avoided, What hurt her the most.

But would she be who she is today?

Life changed so drastically living so far away.

Ripped out of the home **she still passes today.**

Felt like she was with strangers she only saw once in a **blue**

This stranger was different,

But no one yet knew.

She tried to see the light, thinking now she was complete.

To hug and to hold, i have a mommy now

Wow how fun will this be

"Can I call you Mommy?"

"Of course," "we're a family, this is now your home."

A good step-mother is not made, she is built

This task is difficult for most as she has no help

She has to love children as her own that she didn't help create

She starts from scratch, and learns as she goes

She makes mistakes and gets jealous too

To watch her husband care for someone who she has to learn to love too

Doesn't mean she didn't make sacrifices

She loved a man who lost his wife

51

A wife who left behind a child with a resemblance that was so strong

Conversations and pictures of her mom were all gone

Everything was locked away in a case, nowhere to be found

Nothing to be talked about, no questions were allowed

When she asked about her Mommy,

It would trigger a fight

No hugs, no kisses, or *I love yous* were ever given out loud

Buying her love with clothes, shopping sprees were the only way she knew how

Where was the love she deserved? Why was it so hard to give?

She wondered what she did wrong? What if she would have ran away to be safe?

How could she treat her with so much disdain?

All she wanted was the affection others had

If she didn't look like her, could she have loved her more each day?

She created a hate that didn't allow her to understand

THIS IS JUST A CHILD WITH A BLEEDING HEART

Take your time with her, she lost her mom , she not ok

The problem was this child inherited a **Stepmother** who suffered from her own childhood ache

A woman whose wounds were yet to be healed.

There was no silver lining.

She repeated the cycle.

Was this revenge? Or just a huge mistake?

Sadly, it became a child's toxic memory of her early life that can never be replaced.

Mistakes were **not** allowed to be made.

Big Lips, Buck Teeth were some of the horrific names.

"No, that's not my daughter. She is my husband's," was one of her best sayings.

Forced to eat food that made her gag

She had to swallow, not chew, to make it through

Just to avoid the taste

"I made your favorite," **NOT** true

She was forced to clean her plate or hide the food

Pots and pans were on her head more than on the stove

Speak only when spoken to, that was hard to know

She got that face, pinched lip - she *knew* she had made a mistake.

Cries from the room at night, she looked forward to sleep

it was all over till the next day at least

"Mommy can you see me?"

"Come into my dream, I want to be with you.

She wanted so badly to cry out and scream. I hate it here."

Fridays, she cleaned the house all the way through

That was a job a child under nine should never have to do

She would say nothing to defend herself, as cruel words were often said

"Why are Darker skin? Your lips are big and so is your head!"

She had no voice from suffering emotional abuse

Punishments were bad,

Laying in bed for days only to get up, eat and bathe

No TV for days

People would often talk and look with suspicion

There's something going on in that house = but no one dared to speak as she says she's a Christian how can that be

"What's behind that innocent face, that naturally scared look?"

"What pretty eyes you have, are they fake?"

As she Looked at people silently screaming, hoping they would say are you ok ?

No. they change color on different days

she was scared to talk, but imagined what she would say:

"Father I'm miserable, there are things being done to me that you do not want to hear.

I'm being bullied and talked about as if I'm not even here."

If I speak in your presence, the consequences are not worth it , as I live in fear,

Take me home, where I belong, the place where mommy left me when I was born."

hollow aches that haunted her life

she often wonders what her life might have been likeImagining the affection other kids had

How could any little girl endure feeling like she had

Daydreaming about the life she always wanted,

What would she tell the little girl that she grew to be?

Be bold enough to stand tall

you are powerful You are me

Hold on tight - there is a light

it's pretty far but I can see

"I promise-you will be so very proud of me."

A thought that often occurs: why was she even born if god planned this life for me?

Just to be scorned at the beginning of time when she was born?

As she help others along the way

healing the wounds of her emotional scars

It made her who she is today

For that little girl who was never hugged from the person she wanted most

For the father who never noticed she was silently screaming

"Help, help, I'm sad." I don't want to live anymore

If he only knew to pay attention to the girl in the next room.

Her thoughts got so desperate

but thinking to be suicidal was not allowed to be talked about here

in the home where there were secrets that no one dared to speak

Why was he so naive?

Would she threaten to leave?

Was losing a woman more valuable than she?

Would he be devastated and ashamed?

He worshiped the life he lived because he longed for the perfect family he lost

Maybe the pressure for a step-mother became too much more to endure homework had to wait till he came home through the door

He never even knew that this daughter was miserable. or was it just ignored?

She didn't have the courage to say, "enough, I'm not happy here."

If he didn't work so much and spent more time at home, would he have known?

No child should ever know a life that started off just at two months old.

She was the first born out of 5 - the oldest girl

four brothers all from her dad

Boys too innocent to know

all she needed was a promise that she wasn't alone

Her lifelong best friends

How did two end up dead? let's leave a little something

let's come back to be continued to the second part Volume 2

Living as a Young teen girl, nothing changed

No you can't wear makeup it's only for pretty girls

punishments got stronger Bruises lasted longer

What's on your arm, finally a are you ok?

You have the strength, the courage go ahead look up and say

enough is enough! I'm done help me or I'll run away

You made it this far, now it's time take the flight to freedom

back where you belong, to your aunt's arms - where it all started just at 2 months old

She collected stones to piece situations together that she should have thrown

Was it as bad as she thought, the invisible scars from the healing heart ,

she was finally saved at 15 years old, back home in New York right where she belongs

just in time to enjoy the best years of her life

no more suffering, no more tears

You are forgiven it's been over 25 years

A forgiver, a force of light

she is by far the strongest person she knows

She lived to become a new version on her own

she wasn't built overnight

She has a heart so large to love,

forgiving and loving her took a little long

Understanding that she was a person that was also scared

Who is she? She is me, Ia m her

who went through struggles that didn't break her heart

If it happened sooner could she be the woman she is today?

She always had the power it was just hidden but was to dangerous it had to wait

you have overcome You survived

You made it in the fire

you made it out alive

Look up warrior, Your here, You Won

Sincerely, the women behind the door,

All in One Beauti

The artist, The Inventor, The Creator, The BOSS

Christina with her mom before she passed

Christina Fernadez a Professional Makeup artist Turned Permanent makeup artist Born in brooklyn new york and Partially raised in Connecticut . c

She attended Fashion Institute of Technology and Christine Valmy school of artistry In her early years .

Christina shares 3 children with her other half of 22 years a 23 year old bonus son ,18 year old son , 6 year old daughter and new born grandson.

Her First dive in the beauty industry started as a makeup artist At the age of 18, by getting asked by a coworker to do her make up for her son's wedding .

Christina started her early years in beauty as a wedding and special events makeup artist , freelancing for the top makeup counters MAC , Estee Lauder , Benefit ,Philosophy , Smashbox Clinique while also working full time in the Dental Field.

She has also been featured in Kleinfeld Manhattan, The Knot, The Wedding Channel and one of her biggest Proud moments Weddings New York Magazine in 2007 , music videos, various short films, the BET | MTV network and recently The Lifestyle today show for her rose water & concealer from Madeline Beauty .

Today Christina is the owner of All in One Beauti & Training studio located in Bushwick Brooklyn A 5-Star Beauty and Training Studio specializing in Semi-permanent makeup , cosmetic tattooing and educating Beauty professionals to add or start their businesses With an up to date hands-on curriculum in every class .

She also is the CEO of a Makeup & Skincare Line that includes A Professional lash Extension and brow | wig Tweezer line by the name of Madeline beauty named after her late mother who passed away at just 20 years one of her best sellers are the Professional lash Tweezers , eyebrow tweezers, natural brow Pencils and foundation to concealer sticks. Her Products are sold in her studio in brooklyn & Delivered to your door by UberEats .

The Service & Training Department at All in one Beauti consist of All Semi Permanent Makeup | Medical, All lash services , All Cosmetic Eyebrow Treatments, Teeth Whitening and Professional hands on Training In all lash , eyebrow , makeup , hair extensions , Tattoo & Hair Removal laser treatments trained by experienced , caring , patient Trainers .

www.allinonebeautiandtraining.com

Instagram @allinonebeauti

Facebook all In One Beauti studios

Chapter 5:
Unleashing Your Inner Fire: Harnessing the Power of Self

Vanessa Coppes

"The most powerful stories may be the ones we tell ourselves -but beware, they're usually fiction."

Brené Brown

I am one of only five Latina women in the U.S. to helm an international magazine and media company. With everything I've experienced to get to this point in my life, not only do I bring the full depth of my background as an immigrant to running my businesses - I am well aware of the responsibility that comes with it.

I was born and raised in the Dominican Republic, and at the age of 13 I had a clear vision of working in the magazine business in New York City. I could see myself typing away overlooking the Manhattan skyline with its purple hues, feeling elated and fulfilled. I can say owe my love for print to my mom who would collect every issue of Vogue. We'd tare out the styles we wanted to own and eventually had made by our local seamstress.

But life got real and I pursued a more predictable path and become an English Literature teacher. After graduating college and attending design school there, I taught for several years and loved it. I also knew my future held more.

In 2006, I made the permanent move to the U.S. and although I was certified to teach in New York, my love of shoes, and a chance encounter with an executive at Aldo Shoes, landed me a management position at the company, one of the biggest global shoe brand in the world.

After having my first sone however, I went through a bout of post-partum depression and in that moment, I decided to completely re-invent my life. I felt unfulfilled. And that is not how I wanted to continue to move through life.

I struggled through a succession of jobs, and in looking for a creative outlet I focused on what I knew best, my writing, launching my blog *VCoppes.com* in 2009. I was immersed in the fashion world through my previous employment and I created a line of costume jewelry, which landed in the pages of BELLA Magazine in that same year. I was offered a position at the magazine becoming its Marketing Director as well as the Digital Social Strategist, and was further exposed to the entire scope of the magazine business. All this while birthing my second child, moving to a new sate but committed to living my dreams.

So you understand, when I started my business in 2009, it had literally become my lifeline. I was practically alone in Staten Island, my husband still works long hours and I had allowed overwhelm and insecurity, alienate myself from the world. My business had given me all that back. It forced me to get out of my comfort zone, meet new people, connect with women.

This move, while anticipated and amazing, it was cramping my business however. WTH was I going to do now?

It felt like I was back to square one in NJ. With the exception of a few ladies I had met through networking, I knew nobody. And for someone who is so "connected", I remember sitting in my new home-office feeling defeated.

It had taken so much time and work to get my business to where it was and realizing that I had to do that all over gain, - it pissed me off. So much that I shut it down. I would still go to networking meetings, I continued to foster my virtual relationships, but other than that...I was doing N.A.D.A.

I sat and thought long and hard about how to get myself out of this rut...I had to get new clients, I had to meet more women. My usual networking events were far away, the local ones S.U.C.K.E.D. (that's a topic for another book) and this time I wanted to continue to build my brand, but I wanted it to have a strong impact in my community. Why? Because entrepreneurship and motherhood can both be very lonely and I knew that I could not be the only woman who was feeling as isolated as I did.

So I did what any entrepreneur would do: I got a J.O.B. (gasp). It was the kind of job that allowed me to meet women, everyday, with disposable income who wanted to look and feel their best. You know who that was? My target market. On top of that, I got a SICK employee discount, which was to good to pass up.

I had previous retail experience coupled with the years of networking and my makeup mastery and from day 1, I was killing it! Customers where happy and having phenomenal sales allowed me to meet some pretty phenomenal people (buyers, brand managers, etc.).

As time passed and although I was only there for a short time (I wasn't thrilled about a set schedule...entrepreneurship will do that to you), as an innate connector, I became friendly with those phenomenal people.

I had of course prayed for direction and my gut told me getting this job was something I had to do. In that period I met Lynette Barbieri, my ETTWomen business partner (you can read about how we met in her chapter, it's a great story!).

ETTWomen is how I met Jennifer Capella and it has grown and impacted our community in ways that are bigger than us. Most importantly, it became a hub for connecting women entrepreneurs to each other, it has given women a much needed breathing space to grow and learn. BELLA wouldn't be standing had it not been for the love and support I've received from our incredible group.

As the Co-Founder of ETT Women (Entrepreneurial Think Tank) and the ETT Women Foundation, Coppes I am a passionate advocate of supporting women. Started in 2012, ETT Women is a networking organization that focuses on providing business skills and resources. The ETT Women Foundation provides assistance to female victims of domestic violence and emotional, sexual or financial abuse. The foundation offers mentoring programs and educational workshops plus a variety of career, health and wellness services. As a survivor of sexual assaults, I understand the needs of women in crisis and know that your past does not define the future.

In 2019, I had a knee jerk reaction and purchased BELLA magazine when it went up for sale. I founded the company known as BELLA Media + Co. which houses BELLA Magazine, BELLA Latina Magazine, BELLA 360°, and our latest project, BELLA Around Town Small Business Digest.

For some references, both the print and digital magazines are now an international bi-monthly lifestyle publication focused on fashion, beauty, mind and body, celebrity, philanthropy, arts and culture and travel. With an emphasis on inclusion we aim to push the content boundaries a bit, to allow women (and men) to embrace who and what they are. I feel that we in media have a responsibility with the messages that we are sending to young people. Through BELLA, I aim to empower and be a positive agent of change. I am responsible for all the editorial content, securing brand partnerships and directing a staff of 60+.

I do not fear my fire. I am an award-winning CEO, I host BELLA TV segments which bring the pages of BELLA magazine to life along with added exclusive content. I also host the magazine's podcast called *Real Talk with BELLA and am a* regular Lifestyle Contributor on New York's PIX 11 News, I am asked to speak at conferences and schools, even colleges like New York's Fashion Institute of Technology. I take none of it for granted and I give thanks for all of bit of it, every day.

I sit on the Advisory Committee for Women of Color in Philanthropy. I am the author of the book *5 Steps to Fabulous: Choices for Living Beautifully Inside and Out* which covers surviving my sexual assault, alcoholism, and self-destructive behavior. I credit my deep faith for my journey of recovery.

I am married, the mother of two sons and two rescued pit bulls. We all live in New Jersey and they love my Dominican cooking.

I will not sugarcoat entrepreneurship. Since purchasing BELLA, it has been nothing short of challenging in both my personal and professional environments. And I firmly believe that as much as you try to separate personal from professional, that very dance can consequently be more stressful than the situation you may be dealing with.

It's no coincidence that a few years ago I picked up an issue of O Magazine where Brené Brown, Elizabeth Gilbert and others delve into the importance of storytelling and how the very act of listening is where we turn for encouragement in how we live.

You see, stories are the glue of what we are. They stitch together what we become. Our ability to tell them is fundamental to how we celebrate and examine our lives. Sharing our stories reminds us of what we believe in and helps us make sense of the world.

According to neurobiologists, our brain turns into a carnival when we tell our stories; lights switch on in our heads. Through the simple act of storytelling we are reimagining ourselves. This happens even more spectacularly when we hear the stories of others.

We tell each other what's happened to us not only because we want to know we're worthwhile but because we want others to feel worthwhile too. Everything could be taken from us this instant: our home, our identities, our health, our loved ones -but our stories remain.

Our stories are also about self-preservation. When we feel threatened, we run. When we feel exposed or hurt, we find someone to blame. We even blame ourselves first before anyone else can. This is where 'The Deceptive Narrator' comes in. This unconscious storytelling leaves us stuck: We keep tripping over the same issues and when we fall, we struggle to get back up. We tell ourselves lies and we believe them.

The fabulous news is that this is also where resilience comes in. We have the ability to rewrite these stories by challenging these confabulations. The truth is we just have to be brave enough to get down and dirty with *ourselves*. Brown explains it as reckoning with our emotions. When you do, you can change your narrative. She gives 4 steps to do just that:

1. Engage with your feelings. You don't need to know exactly where the feelings are coming from, you just have to acknowledge them.

2. Get Curious About the Story Behind the Feelings. Ask yourself: Why am I being so hard on everyone? What happened right before this Nutella craving set in? Why am I obsessing about what Samantha said? While this step may be difficult, know that the only way to get to the truth is by pushing through discomfort.

3. Write It Down. Get your thoughts on paper. A story driven by emotion and self-preservation doesn't involve accuracy, logic or civility. If it does, then you're not being completely honest.

4. Get Ready To Rumble. Like I like to say 'Let'sRoll!', this is where you get dirty. This is where you ask yourself questions like: What are the facts? What are my assumptions? What do I need to know about the others involved? What am I feeling? What part did I play?

For me, the past few years have been of radical introspection. I've been rumbling with my shame, my blame, my aggression, my ego. I've been reckoning with acknowledging that these emotions exist in me more than I've been willing to admit to myself. And they exist in you -too.

Confronting yourself, your fears, your aggression, shame and blame can be difficult. Getting to these truths is uncomfortable, but it's the road to meaningful change.

"Owning our stories can be hard, but not nearly as difficult as spending our lives running from it...Only when we are brave enough to explore the darkness will we discover the infinite power of our light." - Brené Brown

From my upcoming book, *"Make More Cake: 7 Things No One Told You About Becoming Successful"*

Success: the accomplishment of a goal or purpose. It is not defined by how much money you have, the things you've accumulated, or the certifications you've obtained. It's not until you appreciate what you have, that you'll realize that having more will not make your life better.

We buy things to make us happy and for a while, we do feel happy. Then we get back to our day to day. We go back to what we know: our comfort zone. And then, what happens?

These are the things no one told you about success:

1. You have enough already. Period.
2. Every aspect of your life, affects every aspect of your life. We are holistic beings. When you change one aspect of your life, realize that you are simultaneously changing the whole. You can't change a part without fundamentally changing everything.
3. **You can't have it all.** Every decision you make has an opportunity cost. When you choose one thing, you aren't choosing several others. Whenever you hear someone say that you can have it all, please know that they are lying. We ultimately need to choose what matters most to us + be ok with that. If we attempt to be everything, we'll end up being nothing; that internal conflict is quite literally hell.
4. Never forget where you came from. When you achieve any level of success, it's easy to believe you are the only one responsible for it. It's easy to forget all the sacrifices other people have made to get you where you are. It's easy to see yourself above others. If you burn all your bridges, you'll have no human connection left. In that isolation, you'll lose your identity, becoming a person you never really set out to be. Humility, gratitude, and the recognition of

your blessings keeps your success in proper perspective. You couldn't do what you are doing without the help of countless other people.

5. If you need permission to do something, you probably shouldn't do it. So many people chase whatever has worked for other people. They never truly decide what they want to do and end up jumping from one thing to the next— trying to strike quick gold. Then they stop digging just a few feet from the gold. The ultimate truth: No one will ever give you permission to live your dreams.

6. You earn as much as you want to. We tend to say we want to be successful. If we really wanted to, we would be.

7. Earning money is moral. Earning money is a completely moral pursuit when it is done with honesty and integrity. If you don't feel moral about the work you're doing, then you should probably stop. When you believe in the value you provide so much that you are doing people a disservice by not offering them your services, you're on track to creating colossal value. Our work should be a reflection of us. It's always the other person's choice whether they perceive the value in what we're offering or not.

In my years as an entrepreneur, I learned quickly to stop seeking praise. I also learned that my work had merit when someone cared enough to give me unsolicited criticism.

I've always believed that from a scarcity mindset, when you think that helping other people hurts you because you no longer have the advantage you see the world as a giant cake. Every piece of the cake you have is cake I don't have. Meaning that in order for you to win, I must lose.

Instead, from a perspective of abundance, there is not only one cake. There is actually an infinite number of cakes and if you want more, you can make more cake.

Carve time out every day to grow, improve, evolve [INVEST IN YOURSELF)] —otherwise, your time will get lost in your crowded life.

Elevate your thinking. See yourself at the top. You'll be disillusioned by the perception of those you once saw as idols. Guess what? They are just people, just like you.

Vanessa Coppes

CEO Bella Media + Co

Editor In Chief BELLA Magazine™

Born and raised in the Dominican Republic, at the age of 13 Coppes had a clear vision of working in the magazine business in New York City, but pursued the more predictable path of becoming a teacher. After graduating college and attending design school there, she taught for several years and loved it, but knew her future held more.

In 2006, she made the permanent move to the U.S. and was certified to teach in New York but after a bout with post-partum depression, decided to completely re-invent her life. She struggled through a succession of jobs, and in looking for a creative outlet focused on her writing for her blog VCoppes.com. Then, her love of footwear, and a chance encounter with an executive at Aldo Shoes, landed her a management position at the company, one of the biggest global shoe brands.

Immersed in the fashion world she created her line of costume jewelry, which landed in the pages of BELLA Magazine in 2009. Offered a position at the magazine, she became the Marketing Director as well as the Digital Social Strategist, and was exposed to the entire scope of the magazine business.

In 2019, she was savvy enough to purchase the magazine when it went up for sale and created the company known as BELLA Media + Co. The print and digital magazine is now an international bi-monthly lifestyle publication focused on fashion, beauty, mind and body, celebrity, philanthropy, arts and culture and travel. With an emphasis on inclusion Coppes says, "we aim to push the content boundaries a bit, to allow women to embrace who and what they are. I feel that we in media have a responsibility with the messages that we are sending to young women. BELLA aims to empower and be a positive agent of change." Additionally, there is a digital Spanish language version of the magazine entitled BELLA LATINA, as well as a print version. Coppes is responsible for all editorial content, securing brand partnerships and directing a staff of 60.

An award-winning CEO, Coppes hosts BELLA TV segments which bring the pages of BELLA magazine to life along with added exclusive content. She also hosts the magazine's podcast called *Real Talk with BELLA*. A regular Lifestyle Contributor on New York's PIX 11 News, she has also spoken at New York's Fashion Institute of Technology.

As the Co-Founder of ETT Women (Entrepreneurial Think Tank) and the ETT Women Foundation, Coppes is a passionate advocate of supporting women. Started in 2012, ETT Women is a networking organization that focuses on providing business skills and resources. The ETT Women Foundation provides assistance to female victims of domestic violence and emotional, sexual or financial abuse. The foundation offers mentoring programs and educational workshops plus a variety of career, health and wellness services. As a survivor of sexual abuse, Coppes understands the needs of women in crisis and knows that "the path of the past does not define the future."

Coppes is also on the Advisory Committee for Women of Color in Philanthropy. She is the author of the book *5 Steps to Fabulous: Choices for Living Beautifully Inside and Out* which deals with surviving sexual assault, alcoholism, and self-destructive behavior. She credits her deep faith for her amazing journey of recovery.

Married, she is the mother of two sons and two rescued pit bulls. They all reside in New Jersey and love her Dominican cooking.

Connect with Vanessa Coppes:

Email: Vanessa@bellamag.co

Website: www.bellamag.co

Instagram: @bellamag.co

Facebook: https://www.facebook.com/bellamag.co

Sometimes, our own light goes out + is rekindled by a spark from another person.

However, if you've surrounded yourself with people who always agree with you, you might as well just listen to yourself. The truth is, what you value is an echo.

No one has to lose for someone else to win. A true blessing blesses everyone.

This chapter + book is for you, woman warrior. In the moments on your journey through life + business, you will find a row of closed doors. Here is to knowing that you have everything within you to open ALL of them.

Chapter 6:
By the Grace of God

Jillian Edwards Coburn

O pening my eyes after getting another shitty night's sleep, I realized I have lived to see another day. I followed the same routine: get out of bed, drink some coffee, drop my youngest son Little Lonnie off at school, then go to adoration. Every day in adoration I got on my knees and would ask the Lord, "Why me? When will this pain and agony come to an end? When will You finally tell me how I can make this stop?". This was another day where I felt my prayers went unanswered. On the outside, I luminated light and was seen by others as a relatively happy individual-for whatever that's worth. But on the inside, I was decaying. It felt as though I was being crucified and persecuted because of what happened to me. I kept fighting though. And although I never received any direct messages from God, I was shown subtle glimpses of Him in small things like a cardinal landing on the same tree in the backyard every day. Little reminders that I was not suffering alone, that He was there with me.

To explain to you how I got to this point in my life, I have to rewind a bit.

What do you want? What the fuck do you want? I'm not asking what your husband wants. I'm not asking what your kids want. I am asking YOU what do YOU want? These were words that my soon to be life coach, and one of my greatest friends, Joi said to me in a breakout group the first time we met in 2016 at a Women's Conference in New Jersey. I admired her energy, her persistence, her ability to demand what she wanted and in turn receive whatever that was. At the time, I was in the works of writing my first book with a ghostwriter. Days turned into weeks, weeks turned into months of working my ass off and not having a finished product. I was frustrated and exhausted, both physically and mentally. Each day writing about the abuse I endured in my life because I wanted to share my story to help other women feel less alone, to help others get out of abusive relationships. When I first met Joi, I wanted to give up on writing the book- it seemed like my story, my experiences were not supposed to be told or heard. What seemed like a muzzle around my mouth for so many years after keeping my story to myself, the muzzle seemed to continuously grow tighter and tighter. I just wanted to give up. This is where my mind was when Joi asked me *"What do you want?"* over and over again that day. She continued to ask me that same question on every call we had for the following years. After two years, the book was finally done.

Unbeknownst to me at the time, the ending of my first book was the premise to what followed in the next several years of my life. This is what I wrote:

"Spiritual Abuse is the ultimate abuse because God is where we find our salvation, healing and wholeness. It is through him that we gain our strength to move forward and even share our stories. I believe it's important to understand that this type of abuse is very real, and we must be careful to not fall in."

The first recollection I have of fearing for my salvation was when I became pregnant with my eldest child, Gabriella, when I was 17 years old. I sought out guidance from a priest and told him I was pregnant and that I wanted to have an abortion. He warned me not to get one because I would never get to heaven- I would go to hell instead. I didn't get the abortion, nor did I put Gabriella up for adoption. At 18 years old, I was forced to get married in the church because in my household we were taught to be submissive to Catholic authority, teaching, and tradition. We were taught to never question the Catholic authority; to never create what would be seen as a scandal in the eyes of the church. I was pressured to get married when I was a young adult, to a man I did not love because it was the *right thing to do* in the eyes of the Catholic church. Father Robicheaux told me to do the right thing and because he held this authority of showing members of the clergy how to achieve salvation, I obeyed what he said and I did as he told me to do.

Moreover, when I was married to Gabriella's dad, I would go to Father for guidance and despite him hearing the hardships I was enduring in my marriage, he would tell me to stay in the marriage, to work on being a better catholic, and to "perhaps engage in more sexual intercourse to make things better". This occurred when I was 18-20 years old. As a vulnerable young woman, who already felt like a disgrace to my family and the church, I did just what Father suggested to me. I never questioned the advice I was given by priests because I was taught that they had the answer to any questions I had, that they were the closest humans to God. Why would I ever question their authority? I was taught that they are trustworthy, that they want the best for their clergy, I mean they *devoted their **entire** life to God himself.* When my father was diagnosed with Hepatitis C, he and my mother went to every healing priest around America to try and heal his sickness. Even when faced with physical ailments, I saw several family members who spoke and lived the Catholic tradition looking for help from priests in order to heal the hardships they faced.

In 2017, I met a man named Thomas McVeigh (Mac) Smith, a laicized healing priest. Just when I thought the muzzle that was placed on me was almost loose enough to take off, it tightened all at once when Mac Smith entered my life.

Having always been adamant in my faith, I felt as though some of my previous decisions needed to be absolved in order for me to reach heaven one day; I needed to confess the sins I committed in the eyes of the church. The person who introduced me to Smith was a woman who I was helping leave an abusive relationship. The irony of it all was that I was helping her leave an abusive relationship while she led me to the individual who spiritually and sexually abused me. Smith claimed that he directly received verbal messages from Our Mother Mary. When I met him, I was under the impression that he was a priest- the church he held his healing sessions at boasted about him, the woman who introduced me to him swore that he worked miracles. Little did I know he was asked to stop practicing by the Catholic Church years ago, after the church concluded that Smith was not being spoken to directly by Mary. This piece of information would have been nice to know given that I saw him for eight months, hoping on the promise he gave to me- that he would assist in absolving my sins. He did not absolve them, he mocked them, he used my spirituality to manipulate me, and then assaulted me.

"I have to touch you here to heal the sins you committed when you got an abortion years ago. I have to touch you here for the times you gave your body away to other men."

I felt ashamed. I felt humiliated. He did this for months because he told me that Mary was there too, helping to heal me. That if I just came a few more times to see him, for him to put his hands on me just one more time, my sins would be healed. He told me *just one more time*, every single time.

I stopped going to see him when I realized how royally fucked up the whole situation was. It took me a long time to share with others what happened to me, to share what Mac Smith did to me. Trying to oppress the things he did to me out of a feeling of shame in being so naive and trusting a priest who promised to lead me to salvation. Previously, the world I knew looked black and white; now, it was only gray. I started to question everything I previously knew as truth. Plagued with an identity crisis, I began to lose touch with myself because my entire belief system was misconstrued by the actions of this man. How could a priest, devoted to God, who devoted his life to spreading the word of God, use my faith in the church to abuse me because he felt he had the right to?

I reached out to the Bishop of the Diocese of Lafayette hoping to get a response that stated the church would ensure Mac Smith no longer assaulted and manipulated his victims, like I fell prey to. The bishop didn't respond for almost seven months. His response, when it came, was appalling. After this, I lost faith in not only the church, but myself too. In a state where I buried myself in feelings of confusion, frustration, helplessness, anxiousness, and fearfulness, I closed myself off to the world. Right before I left the town I have always lived in, I reported what happened to me to the local authorities since the Bishop failed to respond for several months. The police did little to nothing, despite their knowledge of other victims that fell prey to Mac Smith. I found myself leaving the one place I always called home. Moving to a place that I told myself would provide healing and peace. A place that eventually provided me just that, after many many years.

According to the Catholic Church, it is of the utmost importance to repent your sins to a priest: it is absolutely necessary to achieve salvation and to get to heaven. In the same sense, when relating this to the health of any woman, it is absolutely necessary to receive regular checkups from one's OBGYN. If a woman goes in to receive her checkup, something that is necessary to her health, and her doctor penetrates her, or touches her in a sexual way that is not consensual; would anyone attempt to argue that she went to her OBGYN because she wanted to be assaulted? No! Or at least, I would hope no one would argue that. The Catholic Church emphasizes the importance of being healed from your sins, of repenting your sins to a priest in order to get to heaven. It is not only suggested for me to repent my sins, it is required for me to do so to get to heaven. The church teaches us to absolve our sins by seeking refuge in the priests around us that can absolve our sins; to my knowledge, the church does not teach us to absolve our sins and be sexually abused in the process. Or is this what some priests think they can do when they provide guidance to vulnerable individuals? It happens to children every single day- these priests are abusing their clergy. Not all of them, but enough individuals are being assaulted that a majority of the population is familiar with hearing of a scandal that involves a priest abusing their authority, or taking advantage of vulnerable individuals.

The years that followed brought me extreme pain, extreme agony, extreme dissociation with myself. Fooling the minds of the people around me, I kept the illuminating spirit that others saw. I wore the big, beautiful smile I have when I am around others. I put on a facade for quite some time to keep others away, in fear that they might realize that something was different about me. I was unable to be present with the people I cared about the most. Preoccupying myself with thoughts that flooded my mind- "Did he do what he did to me because he believed he was helping? Or did he purposely use my spirituality to gain some advantage over me? To convince me that the wrong he was doing was actually his job? His duty?". I noticed how quiet I had become, how timid I felt around others; something I had never experienced before.

There was a moment when the reality of my experiences shifted. My demeanor itself shifted, the way I looked at life changed instantaneously. Little Lonnie came home from school one day. He was very young and attended the new, local public school. He has always been a spiritual being, always spreading love and being aware of the people around him. The words he said rocked me to my core; he said

"Mom. I feel like my armor is coming off being around the people in my school."

What the fuck? Is what crossed my mind. *This kid doesn't own any armor. He's in Kindergarten. What the actual fuck is he talking about?*

As much as I wanted to let my thoughts be verbalized; I asked him:

"What armor are you talking about buddy?"

"My spiritual armor mom", he said.

What the fuck?

Little Lonnie was in public school at the time and after this interaction, my husband and I took action to put him in a private school. The little bundle of joy that I created, my youngest son, was experiencing a dim in the love in his heart, put there by God. Just like I was. This first step, putting him into private school, created a milestone in my healing journey.

At the time, I struggled to even stomach the words, "Catholic School". Why the fuck would I send my joy filled child to an institution that continuously protects men like my abuser? Contrary to my beliefs, the school we chose to send him to doesn't have priests on campus. In fact, it wasn't my son that experienced the abuse that I endured, so why would I deprive him of the security he felt from our religion? Jesus symbolized security to him. Although I struggled to attend mass and accept the fact that the Catholic Church would be in my life for a long time, Little Lonnie continued to show me the love God has.

I spent an absurd amount of time trying to find an attorney while also setting Little Lonnie up for success. I finally published my book, the one that Joy encouraged me to continue pursuing. Shortly after, I found an attorney who would represent me and attempt to hold the Catholic Church accountable. Richard Ducote. The attorney who would guide me through this difficult process. Ducote advocates for women and children in abusive situations and he would be a man who would see me in the lowest point of my life. Christmas was right around the corner and I knew I would see my best friend of many years, Kathryn, so soon. Kathryn's mother lived right down the road from my Uncle Dan, where I was that winter. After months of not speaking, I shared with her that I found an attorney to represent me against the Catholic Church. Kathryn, too, was abused by the same man that abused me. We embraced and she explained that she wanted to share her truth and hold Mac Smith accountable. On January 22, 2020 we filed our case in federal court.

Once the battle began, the wounds in my heart were ripped open, exposing the pain I carried to everyone. It felt as though I was under a microscope that was easily accessible for everyone to judge me.

Attempting to fill my mind with other things, I wrote a cookbook, I attempted to launch my invention, the "MOMMYGOBAG", and I helped pass a bill to help survivors of childhood abuse have their day in court to seek justice when they felt ready to. All of these things I set out to accomplish and did accomplish were distractions to what was on my mind all day every day. Feelings of paranoia, anxiety, panic attacks, insomnia, depression, and even thoughts of ending my own life. People around me would look at me and say "Jillian has it all together! She can handle anything."

Upon moving to this new town, I joined a group who said the rosary every Friday. Two of my new friends ran this group and continued to suggest to me that I needed to meet a woman who they referred to as Sister Esther. *Reluctant* is the best word I have to describe how I felt at my friends' suggestions to meet this woman. At the time, I did not feel as though I had the courage to show face to her ministry. One Friday a woman walked into the rosary with her testimony of returning from a healing retreat. *Oh boy. Here we go again... Another fraud!* Is what I thought to myself. The woman sitting next to me nudged me explaining that the woman sharing her testimony was Sister Esther. I froze at the thoughts and the judgements I was passing on this woman without even knowing her.

Once the rosary was over I introduced myself to Sister Esther and my life began to change for the better. She created a non-profit called the Loretta Home where she ministers families that have lost a child. There is a chapel at her home that she spent an abundance of time making that became a safe haven for me. Esther was, and still is, an angel in my life that I did not know I was missing. The days became significantly shorter after finding a community of people who supported me and genuinely cared about my wellbeing in this new place I was in.

Next thing I knew, it was August of 2021. This was the month Kathryn and I got the news that Smith had died a natural death in the hospital he was in. Kathryn was thrilled at the news. I felt an absurd amount of anger. I would never be able to look him in the eyes and tell him about the hurt he put me through. To stand in front of him with the strength I had been working so hard on having again.

Something mysterious happened four years from the day that I came out about my abuse. At this point in my life, I had made a conscious effort to avoid the Assumption of Mary every year because it was a reminder of my truth. I went to church one Sunday with my eldest son, Matthew, and for some odd reason something felt familiar in my soul. As soon as that familiar feeling sunk in, the priest saying mass recognized that it was the Assumption of Mary that day. My greatest fear was presented to me and I replayed what happened to me four years ago in my head. On my knees before walking up to the altar to receive communion, I asked the Lord to reveal or show me what He needed to show me. The same thing that happened to me in 2017 happened to me on this Sunday- I received the broken piece of the host. Tears ran down my face and I heard: *I love you! Thank you for taking up your cross.* Matthew asked me why I was crying and I explained to him what I had just experienced.

Immediately after church, I tried to call my mom, my husband, Kathryn, anyone I could think of and no one answered. Finally, my Uncle picked up the phone; the same one who lived down the street from Kathryn's mothers house. Uncle Dan reiterated to me what I already knew: that the Lord was shedding light on me and showing me that He truly loved me. This is a moment that I cherish abundantly because I finally accepted the fact that I could have a one on one relationship with God and did not need anyone else to reach Him for me. Uncle Dan told me on this phone call that he wanted to come to our new home to spend time with my family and to say mass at my sons' schools. During this phone call, I did not realize how difficult the following months would be.

Several depositions occurred in the subsequent months. Bishops, the monseigneur, different priests were all deposed; the cult of Mac Smith flooded into my life again all at once. In the midst of this, I received a phone call explaining that Uncle Dan did not have much longer to live. Despite all of the chaos in my life, I made sure to go see my Uncle before he died. Sister Esther came with me to visit him and he shared with us that he was ready to go to Heaven. When Uncle Dan was young, he was abused by two priests. The bill I helped pass in Louisiana allowed Uncle Dan to share his truth with his clergy and the bishop in his parish gave him the apology he had been wanting for several years. Uncle Dan explained that I was part of the reason this sore he had was finally able to heal. He told all of this to me while eating ice cream and drinking a coke that I brought him. That ice cream and coke were the last things he ever ate. Uncle Dan passed shortly after that visit I had with him.

Next thing I knew, it was 2022. It was now Kathryn and I's turn to give our deposition. My deposition was two long ass days of pain; having to walk through everything I went through all those years ago filled my soul with agony. After those two days were over, we had to spend the next five months waiting. In these five months, my oldest son was extensively working through an identity crisis he was having. My husband filed for divorce the weekend before Little Lonnie, our youngest son, received his

First Communion. It felt as though my pain was pouring out and drowning everyone around me; it felt as though I could not stop my sadness from affecting the relationships that I cherished most. My son worked through his difficult time. My husband and I reconciled and are still in the process of mending our relationship. And on May 26, 2022, Kathryn and I's legal team had mediation with the Church and we settled. The battle was finally over in the eyes of the legal system.

I did not agree to settle because I wanted "pity money" from the Catholic Church. I agreed to settle because I wanted to finally move on with my life. I wanted to become the version of myself that I am today, the version where I am not defined by the abuse I endured at the hands of a priest who was supposed to heal me. Money does not buy you happiness. Money does not buy you an apology. When I asked for an apology during mediation, the attorneys representing the Catholic Church had an "uproar" and refused to give any sort of apology. They did agree to write a check in hopes of shutting me up from telling my truth.

Do I feel defeated? No.

Do I feel that more should have been done? Absolutely.

The day the lawsuit ended a weight was lifted off of me. But I now have a family to heal. I know that God alone is the way, the truth, and the life. My heart has truly changed after being pierced so that I could be reminded that we are all created through love. Our purpose is to love each other and to love ourselves. Love is what shows the world that we are a child of God. I am quietly learning that Jesus will heal my broken heart. In my heart, I can clearly see that my story is a testimony of faith and no one will ever steal my graces again. Love will continue to pour out from my wounds.

www.jilliancoburn.com

https://mommygobags.com

Jillian Coburn is an entrepreneur, inventor, outdoorswoman, and mother of three who is passionately committed to supporting and elevating women who have nowhere to turn and living under the shadows of domestic violence. A survivor herself, Jillian energetically assists women living with abuse by empowering and teaching them how to get out, heal and build a life they've always imagined. June 2021 she helped with passage of HB-492, which provided assistance with survivors of childhood abuse to prosecute their abusers in court.

Jillian is the owner of the MommyGoBag. MommyGo-Bag merges military-inspired, functional, and fashionable, "Go Bag's with tactical Field kits to help parents have control over life's situations. Barf...Poo...Pee.. we got you covered"

A successful businesswoman, Jillian founded the apparel line, Reel Housewives of the Deep South, in 2014, producing one-of-a-kind American-made designs for Southern women who love the outdoors and choose "catfishing over catfighting!"

Jillian spends her time on the lake or at home creating new books. She is readily involved with her kids and is the president of Fundraising with her local community club for Lago Vista Women. She enjoys traveling and spending time with family. Jillian lives and works in Leander, Texas with her husband and three children.

I want to thank my best friend Kathryn Thibodeaux, for being the only human I could truly trust through this hell I lived and to my attorney Richard Ducote for being the TRUTH!

I want to thank my favorite East coast rockstars for always being my biggest fans! Jenn, Vanessa, Joi, Lynette, and SuSu! Y'all have no idea how y'all made me ok when I didn't feel ok.

Oh, and you know, my Louisiana gals and Texans!

Esther, Laura, Mirna, Father Ed, Mrs. Lori, man I can name so many more.

My family and my Uncle Dan in heaven!

SNAP- Kevin Bourgeois! Carol Midboe, and so many more survivors I had met.

Thank you for showing me I matter! Because I do!!

To myself for always showing up for those that don't have a voice! I will continue to fight for you!!!

Chapter 7:
Mind Your Words

Sharon Daly Dehope

Mind your words- you talk to you more than anyone else. What are you telling yourself? Seriously!

I'm not good enough!

I'm not pretty enough!

I'm too fat

I'm not a good enough Mom

I'm not the best wife

My house isn't clean enough

My kids aren't on the high honor roll

My meals are just ordinary

I look old

I'm not successful at anything

I'm too tired

I'm not any fun

I hate my thighs, my butt, my neck

Just know, I have said all of these and more about myself. Overcoming these negative words in my mind is why I am a Woman Warrior and you can be one too!

Where is my gratitude?

I know I didn't think my gratitude had much to do with how I spoke to myself- do you?

I found that I was continually saying, these kids will be the death of me. Really? How did I start saying that? I was truly exhausted from doing all the things that moms, stay at home or working moms do.

No one had ever suggested to me, to watch how I was talking to myself- I thought I was being funny- so not funny!

It all started when I realized I wanted more than staying home with my kids. I was a stay-at-home mom, volunteering at their school and working two2 hours/day as a lunch mom, - thinking I was doing the best for all of us.

I then returned to start up my Chiropractic practice again at our current home town. That did not work out and led me to the next town over, to practice there which was- further away from my family.

I was feeling satisfaction about myself, or so I thought. Networking meetings, after school practices, housework, taking care of patients. Doing it all and- with no outside help, resulted in my downfall- almost complete breakdown. I realized again that I was telling myself, "I can do it all. I am a super mom." When I realized, my family was not getting the best of me... I finally left my practice, which I did love. I started substitute teaching to have the work hours match the kids schedules.

I kept telling myself, I wasn't doing my best, doing it all, and yes, I could do better, but never really looking hard, at the cost.

Now, welcome to more hours away from home, less income and with my kids right after work and still housework, homework, sports and no me time.

What exactly was "me time" anyway? The term selfcare was not yet a thing or I did not hear about it!

The famous old phrase, "Calgon, take me away,"- meaning a quiet bath would fix it all!

Never time for that bath anyway. Walking the dog was not even a break, just keep that schedule! Are you tired yet? So now you get my words, sorta, kinda?

Committed to giving my kids the very best I could, since I had very little as a kid, was my goal. It is easier with family support to accomplish this. I started out with having my dear mother-in-law, Nana, babysitting my first child the first three years of running my practice from home. Then with the second baby, I did hire a babysitter, but then we moved and that was the last help I ever had. So, I kept pushing ahead- never patting myself on the back for all I was doing each day. Doesn't that sound familiar to you, too?

I insisted they be in a private school. I had to pay for it, at any cost. It was definitely costing me so much more than I realized. There was a strain on our marriage. Therapy, that did not really help and we finally went to a Marriage Encounter weekend. Temporarily a bandage.

There was still no talk about self-care.

I was so afraid to lose control and trust the One who was in control. That came to me much later on. Things had to get much worse first!

My older son started a private high school and I had gotten a full-time teaching job to pay for it. I had started going to classes at night, homework for me, checking their homework and all the things - now two2 schools- you get it right?

Next, have you heard of that big storm hitting the East Coast in 2012?

Yes, Superstorm Sandy- that one!

It hit us and knocked out our entire first floor, which was only ten10 years old! We had it built when we moved to the Shore area. Where was I going to be a stay at home mom now? The words I told myself after we moved was "why did you go to school, incur big loans, and I wasn't good enough to just stay home and that I needed to work also." Be careful of the dialog in your head. It can really ruin your life, your happiness, your future. Do you also have a bad dialog going on in your head?

Mind your mind and the words you say unconsciously to yourself.

Okay, I did have gratitude for many things in my life BUT the frequency was not there yet and the exhaustion was overwhelming. Anyway, who wants to hear about me and my problems, when most moms were also juggling to make ends meet, right?

I was grateful that we still had a home. Many lost their homes and or cars completely in that storm. Without electricity at our friend's home, we were grateful for a bed, food, showers and eventually a much-appreciated generator- lots of laughs at night, great comradery.

We left our dear friends, who we stayed with during and after the storm, about 10-12 days after it hit. We moved to a rented, temporary home. Not winterized, drafty windows and doors, an electrical fire and a sewer backup all while we were there. Some of our Boy Scout troop came to our aid along with our dear friends, we were living with, and they all helped with the cleanout. We are so grateful to them and their families.

A beautiful soul took in all our laundry and washed and folded it for us for months while we were displaced.

Our Church friends made us meals. I was grateful for many things at that time and so overwhelmed with guilt, fear, and the unfairness of our circumstances.

We finally managed to move back home and continue with the day to day, although our neighborhood took years to fully recover. This was another source of recurring sadness, depression and difficulty being happy each day.

Fast forward through many years of trying to overcome what we went through, but it took a long while for at least me, to heal from this. Our family as a whole and individually we're definitely changed forever. I attempted a session of family therapy after Super Storm Sandy, but it did not go over too well. Three males were not talking about any of it. Are you surprised, I was not!

When life takes unexpected turns, it is difficult to see joy, happiness, and something to look forward to, that's where trust and faith come in. I am very spiritual and this was a hard time for me.

I now know that if I had gone through the healing I needed, I would have handled things going forward much better.

Of course, we don't know what we don't know.

I next stumbled onto network marketing and figured this would be a great addition to my life.

I had been to a home party many years ago, but never thought of it, or Avon or Tupperware as a way to make some extra money.

Just goes to show us that timing is truly everything! A school mom friend invited me to her skincare party! I connected with the women doing the party- I could do this too. This was back with no internet or social media. This was such a bad choice for me then but it kept my interest in entrepreneurship alive for the future.

A few years later, I met another network marketer online and she was the one who started me on my self-development journey. I had no idea how badly I needed this and how my life would slowly (key word) change for the better.

Sometimes, change is so subtle and it takes so much repetition to hear and read what you need.

At this point, I still hadn't done an affirmation or did more than a New Year's Eve resolution which was never looked at again.

Okay to be honest, I had heard of Norman Vincent Peale, and looked at his book- but I did not believe it could help me. It was made for others to grow. That is low self-esteem and little self-worth. These traits are not always visible to others, and sometimes it takes years to realize you aren't seeing yourself as worthy.

Are you seeing yourself yet? If not, look again. I have never met anyone who was taught a class in school called "Personal Development. "

Have you or your kids? I went to many schools as a science major, nutritionist, teacher and Chiropractor in different states.

My journey through this personal development was woven in with being and doing all the things that women do with school age kids. Add in the housework, cooking, driving, it didn't leave too much time for me- do you see yourself in here too?

The only source I knew of then was reading books or listening to CD's. I also had journaling in there but needed more.

Back to the lady I found on social media! She sent me podcasts, connected me to a network marketing guru who I saw as funny, effective and really taught us to come to terms with ourselves. His name is Ray Higdon. I listened to him every morning. He made a video every day for the past 10 years! This was commitment. I learned so much from him, but also sought out other coaches, and was like a thirsty person in the desert. These coaches had me slowly peeling back my layers of self-doubt, old hurts, and not feeling good enough.

All of these coaches were men. Then, I found Kimberly Olson online also known as The Goal Digger Girl, and she became my voice of "I can and I will." Clearly, it was going to take many coaching sessions to end the sinking ship in my brain! There was something about a mom and wife who was teaching herself and then teaching us that called out to me. I felt she was talking directly to me, and she was.

My other coach that I finally met and connected with was our own, Jennifer Capella. By this time I was stronger in my belief in myself and ability to really branch out and start thinking about helping others to discover their healing journeys, as I had.

Thanks to Jenn, I had the courage and desire to book a photo shoot! This was such a turning point for me; a reward for my hard work on myself! It is something that really boosted my confidence and belief in my ability to move ahead with working on myself and growing into a more successful person. Success means different things to everyone. Mine was a need to increase my confidence in myself and my ability to start sharing my journey with others. My hope was and still continues to inspire other women to stop thinking:

" I am not enough"

" I am not good enough"

" I missed my chance years ago"

" What difference could it make now?"

"This is my life and I can't change it"

I am here to tell you that you matter to you! A shopping trip was always my go to when I needed to feel better about myself. An hour in Marshall's was my therapy. Going back home with some items that would make me feel happy, or so I thought, was enough to boost me into a happy mood. Maybe your go-to is getting your nails done, or getting your hair done. How long does that feeling last? Exactly-not long and back to self-hating or self-sabotaging. This can change for you too. It takes the realization that you are worth working on yourself, no matter where you are currently in your life.

We all have had some sort of traumatic experiences in and through our lives. I had many myself. I tried therapy and it did help certain aspects of my life. Therapists can only work on what you share. In my case, I went to therapy because I had mental illness obsessive compulsive disorder as well as anxiety, depressive episodes, and a few panic attacks. Honestly, aside from the therapists, psychiatrists and medication, the best answer was a self-help group like AA for people with OCD. This is not the neat OCD thing people talk about. I wished many times that I had those traits. Obsessive Compulsive Disorder is actually a state of mind in which you are telling yourself lies that are not true. Once it gets started, fear and panic and unrealistic thoughts intrude in your brain. You actually are aware that you are being lied to by your own brain, but the power of these thoughts are uncontrollable. Each person experiences their own set of thoughts. Mine were centered around germs. It was not just being a germophobic person about cleanliness- it was an unrealistic belief that I couldn't be safe if I didn't wash, rewash and rewash my hands in the bathroom. I couldn't fight these obsessions. My home was anything but neat. Clutter accumulated (not hoarding in my case) because I often was afraid to touch certain things. It sounds so unbelievable to see these words written now. Somehow, I managed to continue my life, but you can get a glimpse of why I suffered with so much guilt and anxiety, self-hatred and low self-esteem for many years.

I have endless stories about what it is like to be mind controlled (that is mental illness) and hating myself every day for many years. It isn't easy to openly speak about it but I just know I now have to. If someone had shared their suffering with me, I might have had a chance at healing so much sooner. It's now my time to be a light of hope and healing for someone else.

Another source of healing from my negative self-talk was facing my childhood traumas. I grew up in the 60's, in an Irish Catholic family. We never discussed our family problems...ever. Not...not even in our family, never mind with outsiders. I grew up thinking that having a binge-drinking mother wasn't a thing, until I became old enough to know it wasn't a normal thing. But what could I do about my life? As the oldest of two girls, I was the one getting battered. Drinking went on for endless days. Yelling was the norm, pulling my hair when I tried to get away. My dad worked as a night bartender so he wasn't up in the mornings. He tried his best to be both Mom and Dad, and I love him for it. He was always my hero, my rock, my biggest cheerleader. He is now gone to be with my mom (she passed in 2002) just two years ago

102

in 2020. I miss him every single day and talk to him regularly. Fortunately, my Dad's Mom, my grandma, picked us up every Sunday for Mass and to spend the day with her. She made Sunday dinner and taught me how to bake, cook, knit, and sew clothes. She taught me the values i have today, how to be good, kind, honest and trustworthy. Most importantly, she loved me unconditionally and consistently. My grandpa was another alcoholic, who wasn't too engaging- my memory of him was hard candies. He also worked at Nabisco- so Social Tea cookies were what I grew up on there.

My grandma, Dorothy Daly was like Rosie the Riveter and my role model that women can do anything. Remember this is the sixties. Grandma worked in a glue factory full time. Her only son, my Dad, had enlisted at 18 in the Navy and was stationed on a Submarine. She wore pants suits, she drove a car (my Grandpa didn't drive). She bowled in a league. She smoked cigarettes and smelled of Prell shampoo and Ivory soap. I remember after a shower, she warmed my towels on the oven door. This is why today, I treasure being a grandma to a beautiful, smart, caring, loving five5 year old named Adelaide Rose. Another important piece of my life was my Aunt Adelaide who was the sister to my Grandma. She fussed over my Dad growing up. Then my sister and I who were also her joys in life, along with my Uncle Tony.

Recognizing the blessings we had along with the traumas, the hardships, and the tough times, molds us to the core, as we develop. It is good to spend time in gratitude to strengthen us for what's coming in life. One day after being married to my loving husband Paul for five years, yearning to be parents, I was finally pregnant! It came after the long years of waiting, praying, shots, pills, ultrasounds, disappointments, only to end up with a miscarriage six weeks later. God had a different plan for us. I relied deeply on my faith always. Sometimes it was easy and sometimes it was empty.

The next part of our journey was adoption. This is where I used my mind to manifest my child. I saw myself as a mom, no matter what. It wasn't a term I was aware of the time, but it is proof that your mind can be so powerful. Your WHY has to be strong enough. We brought home a

son, Matthew and almost three years later added Ryan to our family. My prayers were answered abundantly and I experienced joy and happiness along with Paul.

As most families also experience, life will always have challenges. Our resilience to the difficulties we encounter, and along with our faith and our family and many times our good friends help us get through the years.

We as a family chose to move from one home, to another and then again to a different part of the state to be closer to my husband's new assignment at work. We moved to a house that ultimately was knocked down and rebuilt. So our family moved four times within four years- just a little stressful?

I share this because mental illness had already surfaced for me and still we pushed on to have more in our lives. This is not something I now realize were healthy choices for me. It's so easy to look back and see how you would do things differently. Funny how that seems to happen in life.

My point here is that spending time journaling now, can really bring to the surface hidden hurts, unwise decisions, and bad timing which can keep us in a state of negative self-talk make a plan to get up 15 minutes earlier or find time in your day to sort out your thoughts, self-doubts, and practice gratitude for the littlest things. Life and your happiness can improve greatly. Living longer but healthier and happier is my goal and hopefully yours too.

My layers were peeling away but still had much more to go through!

The reason I share about my coaches is that there really wasn't anywhere else to get this healing. Yes, I have had many therapists, but not one had me writing down my goals, rewriting them, saying them in a mirror to myself. Don't think I didn't value therapy- I did and love my current therapist so much. Two different ways of healing which I see working side by side.

So. The self-talk. Healing from and stopping negative self-talk was such an important piece for me. I looked in the mirror and saw ugliness, wrinkles, shame, not enough at anything. I wasn't winning at life but barely holding on. This may or may not resonate with you. It has been actually studied that repeating "I am" statements, acting as if they were already true, can have a positive effect on us. I am a nerd when it comes to research, so this helped my nonbelief. I write post-it notes and put them on my mirror, on my computer and in my notes on my phone. I started repeating them to myself, trying to believe what I was hearing.

My favorite place now is in the shower_ I like to be productive with my time. I also personally find that when these affirmations are repeated while you are relaxed, and taking care of your body is the most powerful time to do this. Any positive thoughts about yourself, or brain dumping about your goals also works then too.

The next step was writing down three negative thoughts about myself and rewriting them in the positive:

One example: I am not a good mom. Rephrased: I am a good and loving mom. I give my family what they need.

Doesn't that sound better? Even if you don't totally believe it, you will feel it eventually.

Another example:

I am always running out of time to get things done. Rephrased: I am scheduling my week to run smoothly with my family.

Another lie we tell ourselves often is, I am so tired. Life sure is a complicated mess but I live in joy and gratitude everyday.

- There are other words that can support our mental wellness. There are actual recorded affirmations which truly started penetrating my mind.
- I actually have started adding my own personal affirmations and making the ones I have heard more in alignment with my feelings
- Journaling using positive prompts on a daily basis has really inspired me to get my feelings out and explore them
- Journaling specifically when there is a difficult time in your life or if a painful memory emerges while you are healing and growing.
- Carving out 10-15 minutes even one to eventually, seven days per week can be the change you need and want in both your mind and your body

I have received so much healing in the past four years especially, this last year. The mindset work we do on ourselves is the most important work you can do. We are always our biggest cheerleader or critic. Why not be your best cheerleader. How do you talk to a friend, your parents, or your kids? Exactly, we usually choose our words carefully to make a point. We take care not to hurt the other person's feelings. We look to encourage, build-up, point out positive attributes to others- WHY not to ourselves? One main reason is we weren't taught this anywhere in school, our jobs or even our families. Right?

I had heard the term mindset tossed around in many posts on social media. I heard it in conversations with other people in my network marketing friends. I heard it from the many coaches I had hired to move forward in my business. I really didn't hear what I needed to do for a long while. Why? I hadn't placed the value on what words I was saying to myself.

I'm really loving to write, to coach other women to discover their trauma, childhood trauma, low self-worth, people pleasing issues. Recognition of the core issues is the key to getting started. Mine were buried very deep and getting through them opened up my ability to feel free and confident and motivated to not only heal myself but to also help others in their journey. Working alongside and inspiring other women to discover their uniqueness and come out with a new happiness, joyfulness and having gratitude is what gets me hopping out of bed each morning! If I can do it, so can you! It takes courage, clarity and confidence which can be obtained with the right leadership and coaching- I am proof it does work and that is why my passion is to help other women through this journey to see themselves as warriors for themselves. One small change in mindset can give you the courage to keep moving forward and living your dream life. Next comes clarity of where this courage to change your mindset can lead to. Next is confidence in yourself and what your life can look like going forward.

Your life is yours, but it can expand and grow to include so much more -at any age.

Dr. Sharon DeHope is a Doctor of Chiropractic, turned Mindset and Business Coach for women

who want to go after their old or new dreams.

Sharon is also a serial entrepreneur, author, podcaster and teacher. Interviewing women to share their stories, successes and challenges are at the core of her podcast and work as a Coach.

As a wife, mom of two, grandma to Addie and fur mama to Maggie the Cairn Terrier, Sharon has a very busy life. The desire to help others has always been part of Sharon's day to day. The platform of social media created a way to reach so many more and led to a strong following there. Learning how to navigate the platforms, the computer skills and going Live on Facebook, were all challenges met head on and conquered, even though they were totally foreign, when she started with just a handful of friends and neighbors. If I can do it, so can you...is the basis of her brand Slay Your Sparkle- at any age!

https://www.facebook.com/sharon.dehope/

https://msha.ke/sharondee_style

https://www.instagram.com/Sharondalydehope/

https://www.facebook.com/groups/slayyoursparkle/?ref=share_group_link

https://www.linkedin.com/in/drsharondehope

Spotify Podcast:" Let's Slay Your Sparkle Girl" By Dr.Sharon   DeHope

Chapter 8:
I Love Thyself

Deborah Ramierez

F rom the time of childhood, we are shown love stories where in every story there is a damsel in distress who meets a man who sweeps her off her feet. Suddenly all her problems are solved and life is perfect and they live happily ever after. We are programmed to believe this is how life is and growing up we have expectations of this actually happening. So we await this perfect fantasy love. No one ever tells the story of how you get a love like that, all the things you must overcome to attain something of so much substance. What is it in life that really leads you to a path of happiness? The problem is most people think happiness is found in someone else and the truth of the matter is happiness lies within. You have to love yourself before you can be loved or love someone else. So after years of not being loved correctly which lead to accumulating pain and trauma from this ever-so-ruthless battlefield of love and relationships here in this chapter, you will find keys to loving yourself.

Dimmed light

As a woman, love is one of the very most sought after gifts. Having it all is not equivalent to feeling it all. Sweet nothings and extravagant gifts only give a temporary high. To have loved and lost creates the strongest of humans. As a woman, we reciprocate love at the maximum capacity possible. We cater to our partners. Making their life a breeze from setting up their day to compromising our own happiness to fulfill their every need while being their backbone. Until when do we bend to the max and finally break?

Being with the wrong partner will make you lose yourself and live in a dark abyss. Dimming your light so your shine doesn't irritate their ego, believing the belittling, isolating from everyone to the point where you cling to your significant other because you've spent countless hours studying them, pursuing them, and making everything up to their standards, working on your every flaw to please them... till you find years down the road you don't know who you are or what makes you happy anymore.

What is it about falling for the wrong person that makes us unlove ourselves? You've over compensated your heart to the point you are unable to properly love yourself or anyone else. I have been there. I know what it is to have lived your life for someone else. Holding onto dead weight. Happiness to you has become a day in which you are noticed by your significant other. Noticed but never seen. You have sowed into your partner and poured into their cup while they are growing and prospering in a garden that you have built around them while you are in the shadows because you're scared to give your ideas out of fear or being shunned. You feel as if what you want has no place in this world revolving around your partner. You eat, breathe and sleep in their every want and desire. You don't feel like an individual anymore... you have lost yourself. You've pushed away people who know the real you, a warrior, strong, fearless, a risk taker, a woman of valor. They just couldn't understand how someone so outspoken and strong could allow someone to hinder them, because they have seen you losing yourself, every conversation with them has just become them trying to redirect you, so you've ghosted them. Isolated yourself from everyone and now your life consists of this person who is breaking you down to the point you are shattered and looking to them in hopes they can put the pieces back together. The hurt place and broken glass is just glistening now off the light that is shining within. It is so easy to feel as if you are so weak to have dealt and continued to deal with this pain.

Find your voice

Deep down your dreams and ambitions are screaming for you to follow the voice that lies within. A voice that's been there all along, but somewhere down the line you tuned the voice out. She was there when you were seven and decided you'd be a journalist while jotting down little stories your imagination blossomed. She was there when you were 15 and decided you'd be a lawyer while challenging your parents for any minor injustice you've dealt with. She is you and she's within. Your first heartbreak and each after, the voice got tuned out more and more to the point you'd no longer hear what you wanted, instead you became different parts of what other people wanted you to be. The scars and trauma you carry hold their own story. Silence is only golden for the person who knows how much your words have power. The pain you've endured has made you bottle up and suppress everything deep inside. Until finally there's no more room for it inside. There's no more room for the negative. The bottle eventually had to break in order for you to remove yourself from that dead-end relationship that was slowly killing you inside.

Breakaway

The Breakaway. Finally free from this partner who God never intended you to be with. Now you have a fresh start. New place. New goals. Out with the old, in with the new, but it's kind of hard to become a new you if you haven't even known who you are in years. Finding yourself is harder than a lot may think. When you lose something in life, the first thing that comes to mind is where did I see it last. So ask yourself when did I last know myself? Where did I leave "me" at? Somewhere in this maze we call life, you have left pieces of yourself along the way. It is time to pick them up. It is time to heal. Find the voice within and cater to it just as you have the dreaded relationship of seven years that only gave you trust issues and insecurities. Cater to yourself as you did the one-sided friendships that were only there to use you as an outlet but when you needed an ear to hear, there were none to be found. In order to love someone, you have to love yourself. In order to love yourself, you have to KNOW yourself! Take time away from all the distractions, and be alone with yourself and your thoughts. Write down your goals and ideas. Your dreams no matter how big or small. Get acquainted with yourself. Remember who YOU are!

It is imperative to take time away from dating when you're in this transitioning state. Many times we leave relationships that have given us unintended emotional baggage and try to meet someone new right away without properly healing first. Looking for someone to fill a void. This happens so often and it has caused a cycle in many people's lives. We can go from one petrifying relationship with toxic traits and on to dating someone new a few weeks later, giving ourselves no time to heal or reflect jumping into this dating pool. This is something you want to avoid at ALL cost because you may actually meet someone who can potentially be a life partner and have all the best intentions for you but since you have this wall you built so high that even if someone dared to attempt to climb it, you'd panic and allow all your past traumas to blind you from someone who is actually attempting to love you. Since you still have toxicity that has rolled over from your previous relationship that you haven't healed from, you will find yourself trying to block the voice inside. This very voice is screaming "let them in" but the voice of your trauma is overpowering and reminds you of your past betrayal and hurt and is telling you to "shut them out"! So you shatter their hearts. Push them so far away and suppress all your feelings and emotions to protect yourself. But is it protecting yourself? Refraining from love? Pushing away people because if they'd get to close they'd be able to hurt you? If you look at the big picture in the long run you are hurting yourself far more than losing them than they could have ever hurt you being in your life. It is NOT self-love, hurting others before they can hurt you, it's self-sabotage. Navigate through the pain. The fear of feeling the same hurt again is keeping you from experiencing good people. This is why you shouldn't date until you are fully healed because you are still accustomed to toxic behaviors. Properly heal from the hurt as the saying goes "hurt people, HURT people" if you do not heal from the wounds and take time to be better and not bitter you will push away people who really had your best interest at heart. The last thing you want is to have pushed someone away and after you have finally healed look back and wish you would have taken the chance with them. Don't do that to yourself there is nothing worse than living in regret and what if's. Heal you, love you, know you. Once you can learn to make yourself happy alone you will be an unstoppable force.

Relight the fire

Relighting the fire inside of you. Start dreaming again. Dream big. Tackle your goals. Start living for you. Do what you love and do what makes you happy. If you've always had your heart set on a business, go for it. If you take all that energy that you were giving for years to another person and put it into yourself, it will amaze you how far it will take you. The more you feed the fire the more it grows, till eventually, it'll be a wildfire on the inside of you that cannot be put out ever again. Fear can no longer reside in you. You will no longer accept things that you don't deserve, you will only seek out quality experiences. Bettering yourself little by little and achieving short term goals and long-term goals. In return, you achieve the best version of yourself. Which will amplify the quality of your life. So breathe and take the leap. Leave behind any and everyone who cannot see your worth. Let them doubt from the sidelines. You got yourself back and you're stronger than ever.

Isn't it crazy how some of our darkest moments in life lead up to the most beautiful things? Who knew a plethora of events so stressful and painful actually would lead up to your greatest victories. Someone is going to love you in the deepest way possible and that someone is you. God allows things to happen in his divine timing and we question why, until years later we are the happiest we've ever been. What if I told you nothing is happening to you, it is happening for you. You have won the war. It's a long time coming but you've succeeded. You have found YOU! At last you are whole again. Not every story has a knight in shining armor, sometimes you have to save yourself from the fire breathing dragon. It is ok to be the hero in your own story. A woman warrior standing tall, ready to conquer any battle to come.

A woman with dreams and ambition to big for the small town I grew up in Panama City, Florida . I am a mother of two beautiful daughters Grace and Sophia. Jill of many trades, Esthetician, Makeup artist, American Kennel Club Yorkie breeder. Owner of Little Bonbons Boutique & Spa, specializing in dog grooming, Dog cakes and pet clothing.

Instagram @littlebonbonsboutique
Instagram @prettylittleyorkies
www.littlebonbonsboutique.com

Chapter 9:
Sex, Drugs, AIDS and the 80s

Oriana Calise

This chapter is supposed to be about my story, it's supposed to be uplifting, inspiring, heartfelt and ...owing the win, the triumph, the pot of gold at the end of the rainbow.

What win? What pot of gold?

I ask myself this all the time over and over again!

I'm still learning. I'm still struggling on a daily basis to not allow the walls I've built to protect myself to actually come tumbling down on me!

My chapter is dedicated to the woman who started the crazy shit show, my mom.

Regardless of the anguish and heartbreak that she caused, she is the reason that I know how to be the best mom! She is the reason that I am here! She is the reason that I have my kids! She is the reason I've helped so many throughout their journey of addiction, without me even knowing just by sharing my story.

I will find my pot of gold when I enter heaven. Until then, I will continue to be a purveyor of good deeds. I will always extend kindness and I will not allow my past to harden me to the best of my ability. Sometimes that's enough, just trying to be the best version of yourself as YOU CAN!

This is for the woman who thinks she is so far gone, and that there is no way out! This is for the woman who thinks she isn't strong enough! This is for the woman who is scared to take the first step! This is for the woman who just needs to know she is not alone! If I can do it, so can you! My door is always open and my arms are always ready to extend a hug.

My life has been a battle since my tush touched the world. I was given to parents that weren't ready to be parents (to my standards). My mom was an amazing soul who was fighting a never-ending battle of drugs. She was eventually diagnosed with AIDS and passed away when I was nine years old. At 11 years old, I was placed with my grandmother who was my saving grace (we all have that one person). At the age of 15, I found a man who apparently loved me and with that "love" came control and an unbelievable amount of abuse. I lost myself. I had four kids with this man and the whole time he had me believing that I was crazy. It was that one day that he pushed just too far and I stood up for myself; enough was enough. I filed for divorce and through the years it was a battle everyday of complete craziness. I struggled to be the best version of me that I could be. I had to find myself again and still manage to put on a happy face.

Years later I found myself and with that, I found someone who respects me 100% and loves my kiddos to the core (he is my angel, I never knew love could be so amazing). Allow someone to teach you that again! The bottom line is the battle doesn't end and I'm still fighting everyday to not allow my past to define my future.

I found hope in my kids that they make me want to be a super mom.

I found hope in love again. It does exist.

I found hope in the world we live in because even though the system is screwed up I still manage to have an amazing life with the family I personally built.

I'm the owner of a construction company coming from nothing. I have become successful because I wanted more and I was willing to work until I could stand on my own two feet so that I can show everyone that a broken woman just comes back even stronger!

If you want something, YOU are the only person that can make it happen.

I'm now and forever a strong, loving, amazing human and no one in this world will ever be allowed to change that.

My best advice to anyone who thinks they can't take it anymore, is to stop, breathe, and think of what you want and make it happen.

Pull up your big girl panties...

Now let's get on with the story.

Let me start off by saying this chapter is not about me. It's about my mom and how the past somehow always repeats itself, unless you hit the brakes and choose a different path.

A long time ago in a land far, far away, called Bensonhurst, Brooklyn (I had to add in a smile because this is about to get very heavy, very quickly) lived an absolutely beautiful, free spirit with a heart of gold named Dawn. Her name was everything that you could think of. It was the sunrise, it was the light of everyone's life. She lit up every room that she walked into with her personality. She was stronger than the sun.

She came to this world from two awesome parents who blessed their kids with addiction.

Dawn- let's call her mom because that's what she was to me. Maybe not the best mom, however she was my mom. Mom was brought here and really didn't stand a chance at a normal childhood, let alone adulthood or whatever little bit she was able to live.

Her mom was an alcoholic.

Her dad was an alcoholic.

Her brother who committed suicide.

Her other brother was a criminal and drug addict.

Her sister who was an alcoholic that died from liver failure.

The odds were not in her favor, if we can quote the Hunger Games.

Mom, despite all of the hardships, never allowed any of this to dim her light. She loved the world and everyone in it. She didn't allow life to place limits on her for anything, that included no limits on drugs.

My mom passed away at the young age of 29 years old. I was only nine.

So some of this chapter is based on letters she wrote to me explaining her struggles. Some of it is based on stories that were told to me by her friends and family, some from my own experiences with her. Please bear with me. I'm just a mom telling you our story in the hopes that this is what God had planned for us. Maybe you are reading this because you feel lost, alone, scared, helpless, trapped. I have felt all of those things and I'm going to tell you I had to pick up my big girl panties and break the cycle. I had to choose a different path for my kids. I almost let history repeat itself.

My parents. They were young, dumb, stupid and probably should've never been allowed to procreate but here I am, alive and kicking. Mom, somehow while pregnant and still away from drugs, thank God, she wanted to change. She didn't want to be who she was. She just wasn't strong enough to fight the demons during our time together. We had our ups and downs. Sometimes we were playing in the snow at 2 AM, dancing in the rain in the middle of the day, and I was skipping school to rescue lobsters and set them free in our living room.

However, sometimes we both prayed that we would survive certain situations. We sat in her friends' house while they were all high, and I was alone in a bedroom scared to death. My mom tried rehab numerous times. She had also decided to just end her life. She somehow would be able to hold an apartment for a short period of time, but only if she had something to prove to some guy. There was Charlie. Charlie was the cab driver. He was cool and he took us to cool places. I don't know why that one didn't last.

Then it was Ralphie, oh my god, my skin just crawled. He was sneaky, cruel, nice and loving all at the same time. He would beat my mom and then hug her and take care of her. He would tuck me in at night and then tell me that the Bogeyman would come and get me if I came out. There were times that he made me touch his nasty body parts and wouldn't leave. I hated him, but my mom wouldn't leave him. She "loved" him because she liked that he provided drugs for her. One night, as usual they were both high and arguing. I came out of my room, and my mom was sitting in the kitchen with ice wrapped in aluminum foil on her lip crying. I tried to ask her what was wrong and she just kept whispering that she was fine and to go back to bed. I heard footsteps coming and I ran back to my room. I didn't want the Bogeyman to get me, but it was too late. He knew I had come out of my room and followed me into my bedroom. He then proceeded to try to touch my body. I finally didn't give a shit about the Boogeyman coming to get me. I screamed and thank fucking God I did (This Was the first time he was going to touch me), or I would have

AIDS to. My mom came running into the room and saw him and she started hitting him and screaming. He was much stronger than her, so he literally beat her. I was on my mom's back with a bat screaming for him to stop. The neighbors must've heard all of the chaos and screaming and started banging on the door. One of them called the cops. When Ralphie heard the sirens he took off, and the cops took me and my mom down to the station, where they called my Nana to come and pick me up.

My mom was going to rehab again, and that exact moment started the 100% guarantee of me living with my father and his wife. (By the way his now ex-wife deserves her own chapter) and it was downhill from there as well ~sheesh remember that pot of gold I mentioned in my dedication I told you about, I'm still actively looking for it!

No matter how hard the nine years were with my mom or all of the crazy that followed, I still smile when I think of all of the good times to this very day. When it starts snowing my kiddos will stop whatever they are doing to call me and tell me to look outside; a tradition I've kept with them. I love hearing the stories live on through family members and her two lifelong friends who still continue to stay in touch. One being a woman named Lynn, who no matter what has kept her promise to my mom, she promised to always try her best to stay in touch with me and she has kept that promise to this day!

I've gone ahead and shared some letters about my mom and even a letter my mom wrote to me- I invite you to read them, close your eyes and imagine the happiest woman with the biggest smile, feel it in your heart then go back and read my chapter again! See what drugs do not just to the person using them but what drugs do to your loved ones.

Drugs have no discrimination, whether you come from a great family or a broken home, rich or poor; no one is safe. If you, yourself have been struggling or know someone who is currently:

Ask for help- it's ok.

Reach out to the family to see if they are ok.

Just try guys- remember sometimes it's as simple as offering an ear.

Dear ORiANa,

I am not a perfect person, and wish I could Be, But sometimes life is just the way it turns out to Be, I Love you with all my heart and will always try to make it Better For us, You are me strength and I need & Love you always no Matter what, It is hard For you to understand, someday you will, and I know It hurts you and It hurts me too, This is why you & I always argue But someday we won't have to and I will Be responsible again, Say your prayers for us and I will say mine and I'm sure we will Be answered. Love Always Mom

Here are two letters written to me by two family members, one from each side of the family.

When the Dawn Set

By: Rebecca M. (A cousin from my father's side)

There I was, 6- or 7-years old feeling like a princess. I was dressed up in a flower girl's dress for my maternal first cousin Jeannie's wedding. I remember twirling around in this frilly dress filled with a petticoat underneath and feeling the prettiest I had ever felt. Entering the age of adolescence, I was intrigued by all things relating to beauty and femininity. It was that night at the wedding hall that I experienced one of my first encounters with being intrigued by another woman's beauty who was a stranger.

I clearly remember being on the dance floor and seeing my cousin Steven walk over to my parents. It was there, at that moment, I was introduced to this vision of beauty.

Her name was Dawn. She had her arms wrapped around my cousin Steven's arm and he introduced her as his girlfriend. She was wearing a strapless sweetheart party dress. I was in immediate awe of her long flowing red hair, pale skin and petite body frame. In my head, I thought, "Wow, she's beautiful!". I could not help but just stare at her, her pretty face and admiring everything about her.

The night carried on and as time passed the beauty of Dawn set in my memory and has remained how I will always envision her,even as an adult besides all the changes that were to come later on.

Dawn and my cousin Steven gifted my maternal grandparents and family with the birth of the first great grandchild, grandchild and the first of my second cousins to be born, Oriana Marie Leon.

The majority of my memories of Dawn after that were ones of happiness. She always treated me with kindness as a young child, always had a beautiful big smile for me, and always had her daughter Oriana close by. Whether in her arms kissing her chubby cheeks, or just laughing and smiling with everyone in awe of this precious new addition to our family.

I remember, if I'm correct, Orianas first birthday party held at Nana's house (Dawn's mother). There was food, family and everyone doting over Ori's cuteness, celebrating. Christine and I played all party long. My cousin Jeannie dressed up as a clown and was the entertainment for the party. I'll never forget her pulling party streamers from her mouth as a magic trick. It is such a great memory! Everyone just adored Oriana! She was this ray of light, just like her momma,that filled our lives with so much happiness.

As the years passed, Dawn's light started to dim and I saw her less and less. I would overhear the adult conversations expressing concern over her well being, but I never really understood just what was taking place. I was just a kid. As I grew up, I learned about her struggles with drug abuse and not being able to care properly for her daughter.

Years continued to pass and the stories of her struggles were more frequent. Custody over Oriana became a huge issue regarding Dawn's capability of caring for her child correctly. I don't remember ever seeing her during this time.

Unfortunately, when I was a teenager, Dawn's battle with drugs took a turn for the worse. I was told she had contracted AIDS and was not doing so well. This was around the time the movie Philadelphia came out in the theaters. I remember watching the movie with a friend, sitting in the theater and crying uncontrollably. This virus was not just a story taking place on screen, it was a story taking place within my family. Most importantly, it would impact my little cousin Oriana the most. She was just a child!

At 8 years old, this young girl had been through so much. Her parents split, custody battles, and sadly, her mothers drug use and deterioration of who she once used to be.

The last time I saw Dawn, she was lying in her coffin. No green eyes starring at me, no big beautiful smile and no warm greeting of her saying hello. Everything about this moment was unlike the Dawn I remember, it was dark, when she was so full of light. It was cold, when she was so warm and loving. She was unrecognizable, when she was this vision of beauty to me as a child. Inside her coffin, a picture of Oriana was placed. This remains such a poignant memory in my life. The idea of my cousin growing up without her mother at 8 years old!? This truly left a stamp on my heart of sadness and heartbreak.

I share this memory of mine for what it truly is. One filled with beauty, and love, and sadly the hardships of life people go through.

I share these memories often with Oriana, and at times try to share them with her kids, Dawn's grandchildren. Through Oriana and the kids I am able to catch glimpses of Dawn. Her facial features, her big beautiful smile and her undaunted love. I will always remember her for the beautiful, smiling, loving woman she was. I hope peace has found her and feel whole heartedly, that she is right beside her daughter, fueling her with the love and strength she herself had difficulties having for herself. I look forward to seeing her again, on a dance floor, in her sweetheart strapless dress, looking like an angel of beauty.

By: Christine G (A cousin from my mom's side more like a sister To Me)

Things I remember about your Mom, who I looked up to and adored like a big sister and best friend throughout my childhood.

She loved milk... with ice. Not sure why that's popping into my head right now, except...you love milk. And cereal. And my Mom's mashed potatoes.

She never ate the ends of her french fries but couldn't really tell me why, when I asked.

She loved, loved, loved to dance!! She danced with rhythm and grace, like she didn't have a care in the world. And she made us dance with her all the time, right in the middle of the living room. It was fun, liberating and a way to release stress.

At her best, she was lighthearted, kind, gentle, and yet more powerful than she probably ever realized. She was fun and hilarious! Random things would fly out of her mouth, no filter. Things that would make you spit your drink out. Apple -> Tree. She brought light, laughter and love with her. She was the spirit of our little family. And when her spirit was broken, it literally broke everyone else's spirit too.

She loved hard. She loved you, her Daughter, more than anyone or anything in the world. And she wanted to give you the world. It broke her heart that she couldn't. It may have broken her more that she couldn't protect you from it.

Our family history is filled with trauma, including abuse, domestic violence, and disease, such as alcoholism, addiction and mental illness.

She never really drank. A drink or two would get her "sloshed", she would say. Later seeing her suffer from and against addiction, in addition to the rest of the battles she faced, was unfathomable but a very raw, real, and devastating part of our lives.

When She found out she was sick, infected by the violently abusive piece of shit she once loved, who had already inflicted so much pain, torment and trauma on her and her child, she was not only hurt and angry but completely terrified. HIV was a death sentence in those days. No one fully understood what HIV-AIDS really was or how it could potentially spread. The mere mention of HIV caused panic. One of her biggest fears was that she would infect you. Or the rest of us. The next several years would be filled with organizations, doctors, tests, her own extreme precautions, and so many unanswerable questions. Life was changed forever.

While she was literally fighting for her life, she was also fighting for you. It was brutal. She was torn apart, humiliated, and demonized with unimaginable cruelty by another person she had loved. As painful as it all was, I think the worst part was realizing that you were turned against her and made to fear her.

Your Mom fought so hard, against multiple enemies at once, to stay alive, stay clean & sober, and to just be your Mom. The weight of it all was unbearable. Yes, she struggled and lost her way becoming unrecognizable, at times. Who wouldn't? She was in pain to put it mildly and so scared. She still kept fighting. She fought until the end.

Reading these letters brought me to tears, I'm thankful to still continue to hear stories about my mom whether good or bad. I know she struggled, I know her life was a battle that unfortunately she lost. However I do know that her struggles did not go unnoticed and that I will not allow her shortcomings to give me the excuse to make the same mistakes.

GUYS BREAK THE CYCLE !!!!!!
Until My Next Chapter
Love Always,
The Girl Who pulled up Her Big Girl Panties
Oriana Marie Calise

Oriana Calise is a wife and a mother of four teenagers who drive her crazy but she couldn't imagine a second without them. She is also the proud owner, along with her best friend, also known as her husband of Caliber Construction NY & NJ, located in Monmouth County, New Jersey. They bring the construction boutique to you! They provide all interior renovation services for your commercial or residential space. When she isn't designing kitchens or helping customers pick out colors, layout and tiles, she is trying to help everyone to the best that she can despite all of the ups and downs.

She enjoys baking delicious old school Brooklyn-style baked goods, and dancing in the kitchen like no one is watching. She is the plan kind of woman. Her life is always an adventure despite all of the struggles. She lives her life with a smile on her face, and her heart on her sleeve; fighting everyday to break down the walls that have been put up to protect her. Life can be good even when it seems pretty dark. Oriana is always seeking the light in every situation.

Her daughter Brooklyn, well let's put it this way, they say God sends you an angel when he knows you need one, and Brooklyn is just that. Her little angel.

Her three boys all hold a piece of her heart in different ways. Her son William (18) is her first born and almost a foot taller than her, works with them since he was 13 years old and is now working full time in their family construction company. Steven (16) and also about a good five inches taller than her, enjoys chemistry and is currently enrolled in AP Chem. He is hoping to receive his doctorate degree in chemical engineering. Christian (12) is just the most loving boy. He has a heart of gold and is a math genius.

Oriana Is always helping others and has recently been nominated for the most inspirational women of the year award.

Handles:

Business Instagram-

Caliber Construction NY & NJ (@caliberconstructionnynj) • Instagram photos and videos

Business Website -

Caliberconstructionny@gmail.com

Personal instagram

☐Grab life By The Balls☐ (@oriana_calise) • Instagram photos and videosinstagram.com

Business TikTok

CaliberConstruction on TikTokIt starts on TikTok

I want to take this time to thank all of the people who have touched my heart in so many ways. The most important person being my Nana. She is the one person who accepted me for me, loved me unconditionally and fought for me. She raised me with love and drive and she made me believe in myself. She was and still is the only person I will ever look up to.

My husband Peter, for loving me even though I was damaged and kind of broken, for coming into our lives and loving us all unconditionally. You are the hardest working man I know and would give the shirt off your back for us. The man that you have become since the day I met you is mindblowing. You are a testament to what a real man, husband and father should be. My Nana in heaven knew what she was doing when she made our paths cross.

To my kids, I wouldn't be able to live a second without any of you. You guys give me the strength needed to fight through every day. You guys are the reason I wake up, the reason my heart beats and the strength behind me breaking the cycle.

I would also like to thank my dad, even though we didn't have a great start to my journey in life, you changed when it needed to be done; now you are a grandpa. You should be proud of the changes you made in your life and the growth that you continue to make.

Most importantly, thank you to God, for bringing all of these people into my life and for leading me down a path to where I am today.

Chapter 10:
Collateral Beauty:
Becoming Her at Dawn

Jennifer Guzman

"You know what, yes, I know I'm crushed. I can't eat. I can't sleep. I can't even think straight. The one thing I am sure about, I have to stay strong for my son.

I don't have time to feel sorry for myself and all this nonsense.

I just want to make this right!"

I couldn't hold it anymore. I had to let the tears come down my face. I was scolding them to stay put inside my eyes, but my tsunami of emotions and beaten face spoke for itself.

"Girl, I don't know what the f*** I'm going to do, but if I have to sell my body and soul, then I will.

I promised my son the world. Do you think I have any other choice? Because I am more than certain I don't. I either swim or I sink."

I was high and intoxicated. But the words coming out of my mouth were out of anger, despair, and anguish. Yet, I knew deep within me that whatever I was going to do, I needed to commit to it because my son depended on it.

"MY DIVINE CREATION"

A woman's power is her innate ability to create and nurture.

I don't think I ever understood that until I had a little seed growing in my womb.

It took me by surprise. Honestly, I wasn't ready for motherhood, but then again I'm not sure if I was ever supposed to feel ready for it. I always wanted to have kids but not within a traditional marriage as my parents would've preferred.

My parents' morals are very traditional and conservative. My father was in the military and my mother was raised by religious conservative parents. Hence, they've always told me that marriage came first and then kids.

I was never complacent to their rules and beliefs. I was a rebellious teenager. Besides, seeing the recurring dysfunctional marriages within my familial generations made me instinctively repel the idea of it. I was certain that marriage was not for me.

I wanted kids but without being bound to the suffocating/asphyxiating chains of marriage. If you ask my current-self about marriage, I'd say "It doesn't sound so bad." Now I'm much more welcome to the idea of marriage, but many of my young adulthood beliefs were a result of what I saw within my family.

April 15th, 2020, was the day I found out I was pregnant, and I was already living with my significant other at the time. The pandemic was at its peak, I had a temporary part-time job working from home. I had just graduated from college with my bachelors. I was intending on applying for several other internships, but I don't recall applying for motherhood.

"So now what? I'm pregnant! I can't even tell my mother, she is going to be furious. Oh God, how is dad going to feel? Is he going to hate me for this? Certainly, I'm another disappointment in his life."

For a second, the thought of motherhood seemed like the worst thing because of how everyone was going to perceive me, "as a disappointment". Yet what scared me the most was the fear of not being able to love this tiny human growing inside of me. I didn't love myself. I didn't date for love, I dated for validation. Who was I to give love when love wasn't given to me? Love, such a vague and foreign sentiment, oftentimes disguised as lust. At 22 years old, I was still a girl not a woman.

My fear of being rejected from my family because I didn't conform to their traditions, and my own fear of being unable to be a good mother resulted in the secrecy of my pregnancy for months.

But honestly, I was fooling myself. My pregnancy was not a secret I could hide forever.

My family decided to take a road trip to Pennsylvania to celebrate July 4th. I decided to join them as I felt like it was going to be the perfect opportunity to tell everyone about my pregnancy.

It was very awkward. My hands were drenched in sweat, my face turned tomato red, my lips were desert parched, and yet I couldn't muster the words to tell them. My demeanor spoke for itself, I was nervous. I would walk back and forth between the backyard where everyone was gathered and to the living room. Until my noisy subconscious self-pushed the words out of my mouth, "I'm pregnant."

My heart sank and their faces were in a state of shock, stagnant shock. For a moment time just stopped and the silence became unbearably loud. They embraced me, and at the moment that was all I needed.

The best decision I made was to tell my family because at only four months pregnant, my pregnancy was an emotional rollercoaster. I went through moments of depression which were mostly caused by every day-to-day arguments and verbal abuse of my former partner. My family were the only ones who brought peace and joy.

I never shared with anyone what I was going through at that time. What kept me going was that I had the privilege to see and experience unconditional love from my parents, my sisters, and the rest of my family. It gave me enough strength to begin and end my days.

Talking about unconditional love, and actually experiencing it are completely different things. It feels very touching and calming to know that regardless of my situation my parents wanted me to know that they will always have my back. They wanted me to know that they were going to support me and love me the same way.

The emotional instability and complications with pregnancy made me feel like my pregnancy flew by. In a blink of an eye I was being admitted to the hospital to be induced. After 72 hours of labor, on December 12th, 2020, at 1:18 AM, my firstborn changed my given name to mommy.

When I first saw him I couldn't take my eyes off his rosy bunny cheeks, and his glazed brown eyes. I held the most innocent and fragile human being in my arms. I just knew I was meant to find him in my existence. He was the missing piece in my life.

I had the most memorable skin to skin moment. I was in awe, having such a tender and lovely thing like my son growing in my womb.

From the moment I held him for the first time, and every moment to follow, has held the most space in my heart.

I was oblivious. Unaware that the beginning of this new season in my life as a mother, would bring along with it many new challenges. It was difficult adjusting to a different lifestyle. I had the most demanding yet lovely infant running my life in every aspect. Nonetheless, I enjoyed every second that I cared for him. It felt as if I was meant to be a mother.

Little did I know that this new journey I embarked on as a mother was bringing along with it a storm of transformation that I needed.

My state of bliss didn't last long. I cannot pinpoint exactly when, but I started to feel and think differently about myself and about my son.

Most times I felt emotionally confused. I noticed that I was having major mood swings. I felt dull and unmotivated, along with other things.

I felt separation within myself and disconnected with my reality. Internally, I felt as if I was shattered into pieces, but I couldn't find a way to put myself back together.

There were many events during the first four months of motherhood that contributed to my emotional and psychological well-being getting worse. I couldn't get out of my own head. I wanted a solution. I wanted answers. Yet, I restricted myself from them because I felt scared to tell someone. I was afraid to be judged.

I was carrying a weight that was sinking me so deep that at times I felt like I was not going to be able to breathe anymore.

No one knew about it because I became great at hiding it, a master of deceit. No one ever saw behind my quirky laughter and forced smile.

Everyone thought I was content.

"SINK OR SWIM"

"Our greatest power is our ability to choose"-
John C. Maxwell

I felt alone. I felt trapped. I felt guilty. I felt disappointed in myself.

"I was right all along! I was not deserving of being a mother"- that song was looped in my head.

Those were the feelings and thoughts that lingered around as if they were just another strand of hair rooted on my head. As a result of those feelings I had adopted the Victim syndrome, a term I identified with for an extensive period of time. I had become proficient in the skill of subconsciously choosing a victim mentality.

The truth is that I didn't ask for the depression and anxiety, but I chose to perpetually victimize myself by constantly professing to myself that I had caused all of it and accepting that whatever bad happening was bound to happen.

It became a routine to go into the shower at 3AM, open the hot water, and get on my knees in the bathtub. While the hot water ran off my back, it was the only time I was able to sob with being heard. Those were the moments I talked to God often.

"God, why is all of this happening to me? Am I such a horrible person?"

"I just can't take it anymore. God, I beg you to just end my pain."

"Am I deserving of it all? Is it a punishment? Or is it just bad luck?"

"Isn't it better if I don't exist anymore?", Yes, I wanted out of the universe. I thought it was better that way.

Except I disregarded those thoughts, since God kept reminding me about my son and the unbearable pain it could've caused to my mother.

Those 3AM moments were when my pain was not consuming me the most, it felt liberating. Those were the moments that gave me back just the right amount of strength to wake up the next day and do it all over again.

"I can go one more day. I got this!"- I was my own cheerleader at times.

Allowing myself to release my feelings was not enough to cope with my depression and anxiety. Oftentimes, I would get highly intoxicated and high because I was looking to numb the emotional, and psychological pain.

I was aware that it was not the best way to cope with my situation. However, it allowed me to survive. I became very good at surviving day by day because I was not only battling my own demons, but I was living under the same roof with one. I was living with a narcissist, experiencing constant verbal abuse, and manipulation.

I wanted to leave, but I didn't have many other choices.

As always, I was trying to save everyone and everything before doing so for myself. I had hope. Hope that for a split second we could be a family, whenever he gave an ounce of effort I thought to myself, "I could change him, he's changing." Unfortunately, he always cared to remind me that "you can't fix what's not broken, and you certainly can't fix what doesn't want to be fixed."

I didn't want my son to grow up in a broken home and without a present father figure, because I know the negative effects it can develop throughout the years. I didn't want that for my son. As broken and unhappy as I felt, I was willing to stay.

I had put up with all of it, up until that night that keeps playing in my head. The night he showed me his true colors and for the first time I was scared for my life.

After that night, I ran away with my son. I went to hide and to clear my mind. I needed to figure out the next best thing to do. The only thing I knew for sure, was that I couldn't share the same roof with him anymore.

Unexpectedly, I found myself in the most broken and darkest place in my life when all I should've been worrying about was being a mother. It was clear to me that this was my version of hitting rock bottom.

This was the point in my life where it all came to a choice. I was either going to continue being the victim and stay at ground zero, or I was going to use this to bounce back and change my life for the better.

This excruciating experience was my point of redirection. I was not going to let any of it define me or destroy me anymore. I chose to turn all of that pain into power and purpose.

As painful as it felt, I decided that the best option for all of us was for me to raise my son on my own. I didn't want this family anymore. I understood that I didn't need to jeopardize my peace and happiness to keep our "family".

So as a single mother and unemployed, I had to go back and live with my parents in their little 2-bedroom apartment in Washington Heights. I also decided to go back to school to pursue a PhD at

Rutgers University. At the moment, it seemed as the only way for me to give my son a better future considering the many professional opportunities a PhD degree was going to bring along with it.

We might not realize that shattered glass shines when light finds its way to it. In my journey as a new single mother and student, I found my path back to entrepreneurship but this time I had a different perspective towards it.

I had a why and a purpose. Hence, this time when I decided to officially launch my first business venture it felt different, I was willing to stay committed and giving up was never going to be an option. Despite all my emotional traumas, the anxiety, uncertainty, and depression, I comprehended that this new journey was also very demanding and led me to: find myself, heal, forgive, find my voice, become relentless in my pursuit of happiness, and grow within my purpose...

It is demanding of me to become her.

"BECOMING HER"

Writing this chapter has allowed me to revisit my old scars, some of which insist to hide very meticulously refusing to completely heal and some of which have reinforced my character.

It is a reminder of where I started in my journey of *becoming her,* how much I've progressed, and how much I'm still longing to blossom and evolve.

The intention with sharing my story is that perhaps, this can be an awakening call for other women to get in touch with their power. Somewhere along in our journey of life we lose sense of our truest self. Within our society, we tend to become a reflection of our environments. Allowing broken people to break us and their judgments to confine us.

However, we all have a choice and the ability within us to unlock our power and soar above.

I invite each one of you to partake on this journey of *becoming her*.

Becoming her commences with a spiritual epiphany where we become willing to reflect, activate awareness, and manifest our inner divinity.

Becoming her is not about arrival, it's about the journey. So immerse yourself in it.

Know that while you are becoming your version of *her*, you will face doubt, uncertainty, anguish, and struggle. But commitment and resiliency are the key!

You might be wondering, who is HER? To answer this vaguely abstract question you must first seek within. HER is the persona, the more you impersonate HER the more you manifest HER into creation. Making HER evolve into YOU.

I now understand that as I am just witnessing the seeds of my resilience blossoming. But don't be fooled, they don't have flowers yet because I'm invested in my healing phase.

At this present moment as I close this chapter and as you read these next few lines, I want you to remember that today is a gift. You are the gift. You are the power.

Everything that we are desperately searching for outside, whether it's love, validation, or happiness, already exists within us.

I dare each one of us to choose to relentlessly pursue the greatest version of yourself. For one flower's awakening, can be another's emergence.

Jennifer is a native Caribbean girl born in Moca, Dominican Republic. At the age of 8 she immigrated to the city of dreams, which is most commonly known as New York City.

Since a little girl, her parents whose highest level of education is one of elementary school, embedded in her the value of education as a roadmap to success. As a first-generation Latina college student from an economically & socially disadvantaged family, the odds of graduating college were narrow. However, she owes her success to the efforts, sacrifices, support, and guidance of her parents along with the partnerships she established with peers and mentors. She now holds degrees from Lehman College & most recently she obtained her Master's from Rutgers University.

From solely being interested in pursuing a research-oriented career in Material Chemistry, her

active efforts in addressing issues of underrepresented groups in STEM and Finances

motivated her to commence her journey of entrepreneurship in 2018.

In 2021, she officially launched her first business becoming the first in her family to become a

CEO & founder. She started her own Tax Preparation & Accounting Firm, Bright Tax Services Corporation where she focuses on empowering and improving the lifestyles of the Latino community by highlighting the importance of prioritizing Financial

Wellness. She aims to accomplish this by providing accessible and high-quality financial services.

Even when considering the taboos and stigmas surrounding mental health, Jen passionately

vocalizes her experience as a survivor of domestic violence and as a mother overcoming her severe postpartum depression and anxiety.

She is a mother to a beautiful 2-year-old. As a single mother, her main priority is being a present

mother and managing her time properly to nurture her relationship with her son.

Outside of entrepreneurship & motherhood, Jen enjoys working out, traveling, trying new foods,

reading personal development books, and connecting with other powerful and passionate women. Oftentimes, she indulges in watching horror movies.

Most recently, Jen is developing a consulting and financial literacy platform targeting Latina

Women which she expects to share with the world later on this year. Through her platform, she

hopes to enlighten Latina women to become the first wealth builders.

Writing this chapter has been the hardest yet most rewarding experience in my life. I couldn't end this without first thanking God. He knew that I was ready to share with the world about such a pivotal season in my life. He intended me to tell my stories so that other women out there in the world could be empowered.

I'm eternally thankful to Jennifer M. Capella for this opportunity. It is an honor to share this experience with a collective of powerful women that love, respect, and uplift each other.

To my sisters Nilly and Gigi, you are both amazing souls and I am blessed to have you both part of my life. The way we connect with each other is invaluable. We are more than sisters. We were meant to find each other in our destinies.

To my mother Teresa, who I have seen sacrifice her peace, health, and sanity for the wellbeing of the family. I am honored to be your daughter. You are one in a million and I wish there were more people like you in the world. You are selfless. You are my superhero. God chose the perfect mother for me and now that I am a mother I realize that you are more special than I already thought. I now feel a deeper love for you, I respect you more, I admire you more, and I feel that there is no way I can thank you for all that you do for me.

Finally, to my son who has completely transformed my life in unexpected ways. Everyday you teach me something new about motherhood and myself. You uplift me and make me smile even on my cloudiest days. You are my divine gift and I have sworn to protect you forever.

Regardless of the short distance that once separated us, Tu siempre eres y seras la luz de mis

ojos.

Chapter 11:
Separation is the New Diet

Nastasya Rose

Beginning

It was two a.m.

I was restless.

No matter what, I couldn't sleep.

It was the weirdest thing.

None of it was planned. But my soul knew it was time.

We thought about it for years. Talked about it for years.

But after our launch shoot with my team, I saw the vision of the future. And I knew it was time.

I had to eliminate what was in my way of moving forward in my truth.

I have to take a stand at the next level for this success to continue.

I was nowhere near ready. But it was time.

I texted our therapist to make sure she was definitely showing for our session.

Because deep down, my soul knew before I did, what I was about to do.

And I knew I needed the best support to do it.

I went to sleep, and woke to my therapist's confirmation of our session still happening at ten a.m.

Then, one more occurrence happened confirming even more it was time.

I told my son what I was about to do. We cried and held each other.

I told his teacher what I was about to do. I cried, and she hugged me.

Then, finally, ten am came. The therapist started our session with me and my fiancé.

Our therapist asked, "What am I witnessing here?"

Before my fiance could even speak, I cut him off, talked over him and said,

"You're witnessing a break up."

Middle

Eight years of loving him.

Eight years of going through hell and back with him, and we survived.

So why the hell was I even doing this?

Welp. This was why.

I was done with just surviving.

Eight years and we tortured each other in secret.

Even worse, I kept witnessing gaslighting of what shouldn't be gaslit.

No matter how hard I tried, I just couldn't accept it.

How can you survive infidelity, sexual assault from another man, and losing who you thought was a best friend in the family in back-to-back episodes and still live a normal life?

Even worse, this wasn't the first time I survived assault.

I've been assaulted every ten years since the age of four. So this assault just put the icing on the cake.

It put me in a level of rage I've never lived in my life, nor would I wish on even my worst enemy.

I wanted to kill my assaulter this time. More than the others.

Millions of times I contemplated getting the gun for revenge.

Now I just consider it for protection.

Then, the next thought would be,

"Why am I not allowed to be exotic without being an object of prey for the predator?

Why am I cursed like this? What's the point of living if ten years from now this is just going to happen again?

Nas just end your life. Just do it now. No one is going to care. Possibly, no one will even notice. Even if they do, they'll just forget in a week. It's okay."

Then. I remembered my son.

My gorgeous son. My miracle.

Due to my trauma, I never thought I'd be blessed enough to be a mother.

He's my angel. Him being created saved my life.

Once thinking of him, I knew I had to change the narrative.

No way I could do that to him. I have to teach him better so he knows how to be great. Even greater than me.

Then, the second thought that came into my head... my clients.

Oh, Lord. The beautiful survival of my clients and their trauma deserves a chronicle of books itself.

What in the world would I be teaching them by going against God's Purpose for my life?

Deletion can be contagious if we're not careful. Look at the history of the topic.

We must continue in honor of those we've lost, and in honor of those who fight so hard every day to stay alive.

After thinking of them, and my mentees, I thought to myself, no way could I ever do that to them.

They're my world. I have to show them better.

Their purposes were and are too powerful. They're meant to be accomplished.

I have to stick around for them.

Third? My father. How in the world could I leave him after everything we've survived?

We still have our statement to be made. After everything.

Then finally, I thought of myself.

How could I possibly look at my Maker after going through with deletion and expecting to still be allowed in His Kingdom?

When I know what it says in the Written Word?

I cried on my knees, begged God for His forgiveness, and promised to move forward in His Truth best I can.

This is why I moved forward with the separation. There's no way I could fake a "normal" relationship with my fiancé when the incidents during and within our bond were torturing me in these ways.

I had to tell these demons they were no longer welcome, and show it with my strike.

What did this separation journey look like?

I'm sure at this point of reading, you may wonder, 'how the heck did this woman go from thinking like that, to being relentless in the ways she is today?"

First thing? I had to choose to stop caring about anyone's judgment.

During this separation, I was also dealing with such heartbreak within my work team.

So many ways I was internally crying for help and the most important team members never knew.

When you do the type of work like I do, you need extreme uniqueness when it comes to support from your team.

Think about it. I serve thousands now in VIVE™. And the hundreds of women I've mentored? Who's survived the heaviest trauma you can possibly imagine?

Where do you think that traumatic energy goes?

In me.

I need a team who is supportive on a different level for me as I detox that type of energy on a daily basis out of my body so we can be successful together within our project work.

I had to stop caring about judgment so I could create that dream team.

Then, I had to develop the dream team. I'm proud to say after five years straight focusing on that development, I'm almost there.

Next? I needed to create my support system for the personal side of my life.

I had to finally find my dream therapist.

I'm so proud to say after 21 years, I've finally found her. I was extremely intentional in this one.

I need one of the most strong therapists to support me in my professional work and to support me through the trauma I've survived since infant years.

To finally get me out of my house. Ever since the assault, I've been terrified to leave.

To help me create protocol so I'm not worried my body will be disrespected again ten years from now. This is essential so I'm not tempted for deletion, but living for my son and those I love.

A disclaimer for my mentees reading this - if you ever wondered how I'm so good at mentoring you to not self-delete for those who experience this, now you know why. Like I always tell you. It's all about the systems. I say this for a strong reason. Sometimes, those systems can literally keep you alive.

Finally, I needed to rediscover who I truly am after all this, and solidify my boundaries to support my truth.

And for the finale, I needed to create a system where I stood my ground on the toxicity that could no longer exist in my connection with my fiancé.

There had to be a bulletproof system where we definitely walked through life together in confidence. Where we truly are a loving partnership.

If that couldn't happen, we could never be.

I'm surprised to say, me and my fiancé are a huge exception to the rule.

Separation became the new diet.

When I thought he wouldn't make the cut, he amazed me.

But it was only because I first began the work of reframing the story within myself.

Ending

Psychological, emotional and physical abuse is unacceptable.

Denial of mental help needed is unacceptable.

Infidelity is unacceptable.

Narcissism is unacceptable.

Secret mistreatment and manipulation is unacceptable.

Misaligned support in sexual assault survival from another man is unacceptable.

Misusing the word rape is unacceptable.

None of this generational demonic work is acceptable.

I saw no one putting an authentic and loving end to any of this.

Not in ways where there could be true change.

If we were to continue together, we had to take a stand to these things in unison and in healthier ways. I get that it's not easy to do. But still. Not an excuse.

I thank God we chose to be the exception to the rule.

There was something that mattered more. More for us, our son, our heritage.

Something that should've started in action generations ago.

Something we knew could only get started once choosing to stand together.

That something was, and is....

If we don't start standing for removing and killing these generational demons terrorizing our lineages... when will we?

Even if I die earlier than expected because I tell these demons they were never welcome here and they get so upset they don't let me continue my Purpose,

even if I have to watch my most gorgeous son from heaven, at least I know I didn't disobey God and lived my Purpose in full.

I don't want to die. I want to live long.

However, we never know of tomorrow. That's why we get told to live today. I can only give my best in the present with all my heart as best I can.

If I die, I die knowing I finally did what no one before me could do.

I would know I cared for the safety, success, and livelihood of my son, and all survivors, with all my being.

He could see what I left behind, and know how to carry the torch to see it through.

And even more beautifully, the thousands of women I mentor can see what it looks like when we stand in our truth, unafraid, and create generational change.

I can see the vision of living long and living my purpose in full.

And I can see the vision of being killed by my assaulter or by anyone envious of me.

I choose to stand for the former.

Because when I go, I want the story told when I was alive I looked at our generational demons right in their satanic eyes and said,

"Your lease is long overdue. Your eviction has arrived. It's time for you to go."

Nastasya Rose, Founder, CEO & Master Coach of VIVE™

Nastasya Rose is the Founder, CEO & Master Coach of VIVE™, a private practice for creators, entrepreneurs and celebrities helping them succeed in their visions while keeping their energy and mental health, first founded in 2010. She is a Board Certified Professional Coach and Energy Leadership Master Practitioner running the vision of her practice since it first came to her at 14 years old after her mother's mental illness diagnosis.

Holding near 20 certifications, a Bachelor of Science in Addiction Counseling from Grand Canyon University, and currently studying her Master of Science in Clinical Mental Health Counseling with emphasis in Trauma, Nastasya Rose aids her clients in igniting their visions while keeping their energy and mental health first. She helps creators and creative professionals scale to the 7-10 figure marks and beyond with the mix of Energetics, Clinical Therapy, and Business Strategy & Systems so their visions can succeed well enough to not only make it in the present, but to pass forward as they desire to generations to come.

After surviving her own trauma experiences, she wanted to run her own practice where she can connect with her clients in ways not provided in the business and mental health industries.

She's known for her award winning VIVE DETOX™ division featuring her signature service, Rock the Breakthrough™, a one-year mentorship experience where she aids her clients to succeed in igniting their visions to consistent $10-$20k months while keeping their energy and mental health first. She's preparing for multiple exclusive projects over the coming years including reopening her location after years of healing from surviving sexual assault.

Aside from this work, Nastasya Rose has mentored top celebrities, entrepreneurs, and C-Suite Executives 1:1 in full confidentiality. She's also evolved into corporate contracts with franchises and health care practices to aid their patients in the best of success with their treatment plans for better mental health.

She's also in development of her VIVE TM ☐ Foundation non profit organization where she'll be giving back with her team to survivors of trauma, assault, and abuse.

Nastasya Rose is here and ready to make a difference in our community mentoring creators and entrepreneurs to greatness for the lives they wish to live.

To learn more about her company VIVE™☐, feel free to visit her site at whyvive.com.

In closing, a quote from our Founder:

"The road's not easy, but the steps are simple.

Just keep walking."

To my son. You are the reason this chapter was able to be written. I do this generational healing for you. So you can see what it looks like when we fight our demons not meant to exist in our lineage. We are spiritual warriors. May you be inspired to carry the torch when your time comes.

To those who made an impact on me - Stephen 'Twitch' Boss and Jason David Frank. Twitch was a being whom inspired me. Jason was a being I actually knew. I only pray I can show the example of what it can look like when our souls are actually felt, and our voices actually heard.

167

Site the VIVE

IG Nastasya Rose ☐ Speaker Mentor Lyricist (@nastasyarose) • Instagram photos and videos / VIVE ™ (@whyvive) • Instagram photos and videos

FB https://www.facebook.com/nastasyarose/ / https://www.facebook.com/whyvive/

FB Group: VIVE Lounge™

LinkedIn https://www.linkedin.com/in/nastasyarose/ / VIVE™ | LinkedIn

Founder and Master Coach of

VIVE **FOX** BELLA **BRAINZ.**

as featured in **Entrepreneur Forbes**

Chapter 12:
Forty-Eight

Wendy Murphy Knox

This chapter began in February 2022 on a picturesque hillside of Tamarindo, Costa Rica where I was excited to get to know this wonderful group of ladies on my first ever solo trip outside of the United States! For me, this was the trip that I had been dreaming about for at least twelve years after reading Eat. Pray. Love. by Elizabeth Gilbert in 2010. After the past several years of working myself until I was completely burned out in hospitals across the United States, I booked this yoga retreat as a 48th birthday present to myself because in my mind I had finally earned it (one of my bucket list goals). A trip filled with yoga, meditation, girl talk, healthy eating, and new conversation was just what I needed after two long years of nursing the sick back to health or watching death consume them from this ongoing coronavirus pandemic. This trip was full of intimate conversations about our hopes, dreams, aspirations, and goals. I was able to be vulnerable with these ladies; because who are they anyway? and most likely I will never see them again (having no idea we would form lasting friendships and bonds).

Who was I kidding? This chapter was inspired to be written by these ten ladies who made such an impression on me during this once in a lifetime trip; although this chapter actually began over 20 years ago when I was much younger. A million "thank you's" could never be enough for the encouragement, empowerment, and vulnerabilities that were freely offered on this tropical retreat. I should add an extra special "thank you" to Toni, the retreat host, for recognizing my 48th birthday with a cake, candles, and the birthday song. I am not really sure that I can remember the last time that happened and it meant so much to me! I am not sure if these ladies realize just how much they motivated me to start facing the challenges of my goals, but they unlocked something inside already rousing inside my soul. While writing this chapter, I can't help but think about what Edison once said, "If we did all the things we are capable of, we would literally astound ourselves." This was such a fitting quote as Olga and I sat on our mats in the outdoor yoga shala with a stunning view while tossing out ideas, sweat and tears. This woman that I just met personally challenged me to reach way outside of my comfort zone to meet two of my goals; writing a book and starting a business. Just in that short time our friendship became a part of me that I will always cherish. After I returned home from my birthday trip, my smart, witty, beautiful, new friend Olga sent me a stunning framed photo of a dreamcatcher on a piece of driftwood that she captured while walking along the beach of Costa Rica. This beautiful reminder of our special friendship hangs right above my nightstand by my bed. This piece of driftwood signified to me that at that exact moment, I was in the place where I was meant to be. I questioned myself often in those days leading up to boarding the plane to Costa Rica about taking a trip to a country I'd never been to and meeting a group of women that I had never met; and I am so glad that I didn't back out. You see, there were bonds created on that trip that will be treasured for years to come; all while we were attempting to balance our body, mind and soul with the art of meditation. I mean how many times can one say, "I participated in a yoga class focusing my body, mind and soul with something as massive as a volcano in the background?" This will not be my last yoga retreat with Toni!

I have set many goals for myself throughout my life. I have achieved many of those goals, although most did not come without disappointment and/or setbacks. Like many, my mindset has been on pursuing these hopes, dreams and goals at just the right time, but what I have found is that there is no perfect time and for me, I needed to balance my own unrealistic expectations of myself with what the outside world expects of me. Just in writing this chapter I experienced many obstacles and yet here I am, reaching another goal. It is simple: those with a vision that set a goal WILL experience shortcomings and setbacks and the plan may be altered; but those who persist will increase their self-confidence and build perseverance for future goal setting (dreaming) and goal getting (achieving).

The truth is, in my earlier years, I didn't know I was setting goals for myself. I was just dreaming about these things that I hoped to one day achieve in life. I do know that I was set on changing the course of my life. I wanted to be more and do more. I just didn't know how that would come about. I'm not even sure that I truly understood what setting a goal was until one day while I was sitting in one of my nursing classes somewhere between the ages of 32-34 years old. We were learning the difference between short-term goals versus long-term goals for our patient care plans (a long and dreadful document that was graded and carried a heavy weight for the semester that had the entire class stressed out-all nurses will understand) when my own light bulb started flickering. I was literally in the midst of attempting to achieve a goal that I had set for myself 15 years earlier without the true knowledge that it was even a goal. Becoming a nurse was something I had wanted to do since before I graduated high school. I just never had the courage to attempt it. I graduated high school in June of 1992 and immediately enrolled in college classes. I can remember touring through the small college in my hometown like it was yesterday (almost thirty-one years ago). I quickly learned that I was tired of school and dropped out of college receiving an "F" in all four of those college courses. In 2001, a difficult time in my life motivated me to find out exactly what I was capable of so I enrolled in one college class at a time until I realized that I could handle it with a family and a full-time job.

Anyway, at that moment-sitting in class, I realized that in order to achieve future goals, I would need to start small and dream big. In December 2008, at the age of 34; I graduated with my first college degree. Not only did I graduate, I graduated as the Salutatorian. I don't say this in a bragging manner but rather just to say that I went from being in the lowest part of my high school graduating class to number two in my college class and what a feeling of achievement it was!

It hasn't always been easy; actually, it's never been easy and has always been more challenging than not. I did it and so can you! Start making your goal setting and goal getting. Write it down on paper, make a note in your phone, or type it on your computer immediately!

In thinking back on my life and accomplishments, I have created this list of goals that I began setting for myself after the light bulb came on for me. Some of these are short-term goals while some of them are long-term goals; several of them have been achieved while others are still being worked on.

1. My number one goal from the time I conceived my beautiful daughter Kayla, was to be the best

mom that I could be. I truly wanted to be the mom that she looked up to, could depend on, and to be an inspiration for her when setting her own goals. This has given me a complete sense of accomplishment and fulfillment. She is twenty-eight, is a registered nurse and is able to pay her own bills. This, I waited patiently on while she was in college so I could start spending the money I made on me. I am proud of her accomplishments and she brings me joy on a daily basis. Her most recent goal getting is making me a Mimi and I couldn't be more thrilled. September 2023 can't get here soon enough!

2. Be a good wife. Having a family was important to me. I wanted the white house with the picket fence. I had the white house with the husband, daughter... and the dogs, cats, squirrels, hamsters, gerbils, birds, turtles, and all the sand fiddler crabs you could imagine. Having a stable home for my daughter was a priority. I wanted her to have a safe and secure space to grow up. Although we divorced when she was nineteen, we were able to give her a place where she could be a kid and enjoy life. And for that I am thankful.

3. Improve my self-esteem. I was not sure how this would happen as I had very little. And little did I know that this one would take a lot of proving to myself that I could accomplish it....and I did! Graduating nursing school was extremely helpful.

4. Become a better person. As a young adult I didn't necessarily think I was a bad person, I just didn't think I was the best version of me. I wanted to be better. I wanted to do better. And I wanted to live better. I craved positivity. I promised myself that when I became a mom, I

would speak and teach my daughter positive words and ways. Ultimately what I have learned is that I want to be better tomorrow than I was today. I want to do good for myself and for others. Encourage others to pursue their dreams (I always say "the sky is the limit"), put a smile on their face, love them unconditionally and motivate them to be their best self, whatever that may be. Life isn't always sunshine and rainbows and certain situations can make this more difficult to do.

5. Be the best employee I could be. I want to exceed and do my best at whatever job I accept. I remember working in the billing department at the local hospital as a reimbursement specialist (this was my first job in healthcare as a temp employee). My job was to go through the patients' account and figure out if the credit was due back to the patient or the insurance company. Every Monday morning my partner and I would run a new report and the race was always on until Friday trying to clear the report. I wanted to get as far as I could through that report every single week. I loved the challenge. It has been the same for every position I've had; it gave me a sense of pride and self-satisfaction.

6. Become a Nurse. Nursing school was a beast of a different kind. Aside from raising my daughter, this was the hardest thing I have ever done. It challenged me, it changed me as a person, and it completed me. I completed my Associate Degree in Nursing in 2008, Bachelor of Science in Nursing in 2012 and my Master of Science in Nursing with a specialization as a board-certified Family Nurse Practitioner in 2020! For someone that never excelled in any grade in school, this has been my second

greatest accomplishment only behind raising a beautiful and smart daughter. When I was in college, it was important to me to work hard and do my best. I needed to prove to myself that I could make the grades that I wanted; the ones I could never make in high school because I never knew how to study. This was a major accomplishment for me and I honestly never imagined that I would be where I am today as a board-certified family nurse practitioner.

7. Become a travel nurse. This was my single goal of becoming a nurse. I remember telling my family and friends this specific goal. Oftentimes just speaking a goal out loud encourages us to make it happen, I truly believe this with all of my heart. I started travel nursing in 2013 and completed my 20th travel contract in February 2022. Although it was something I had planned to do, one of my dear, sweet patients actually encouraged me to take the leap into travel nursing when I did. He encouraged me to travel while I could as he had planned to one day and just never had the chance for many reasons. He regretted that he was never able to and said, "young lady, if you have this opportunity, please don't give it up." I remember those words like it was yesterday and it has been ten years now. You will hear more about him later in this chapter as he is someone who inspired me through his time of tragedy.

8. Travel abroad for a medical mission trip. This one hasn't actually happened yet although I did travel to Guam as a travel nurse during the COVID-19 pandemic in 2021 where I worked for six months as a bedside nurse. I worked at Guam Memorial Hospital Authority, a small public hospital that has served the island for

over a half a century. It has by far been one of the most treasured times of my nursing career. This is where I must tell you that Guam is a small United States island territory in Micronesia located in the Western North Pacific Ocean and is known for its tropical beaches, Chamorro culture, Spanish colonial heritage, and playing a significant role in World War II. It is situated a whopping six-thousand miles from the coast of San Francisco, and a twenty-four-hour flight from South Carolina. So many people that I have encountered have no knowledge of the existence of this breathtaking gem. You also probably didn't know that Mount Lamlam on Guam is technically the tallest mountain in the world because of the Marianas Trench. This beautiful island is home to some of the most kind, generous and selfless people that I have ever met. The people of Guam befriended me, took me to dinners, were my tour guide around the island, fed me lunch at work, took me on hikes, made sure I didn't spend Mother's Day alone and invited me to family celebrations. The people of this island were what I desire to be in two words; humble and kind. The friends that I made in Guam will forever hold a special place in my heart.

9. Truly find myself. Reflecting and deciding what is important in life has been a game changer over the past ten years. Self-discovery, self-care, and self-love has improved my life in many ways. This is an important part of our life journey as we can often lose sight of our own needs and wants when we have others to care for. It helps us to find what our purpose in life may be. This one is still a work in progress as I am always learning new things about myself. I

am a nurse so being an encourager, and a comforter to others comes naturally for me. When I say, "I hope you have a good day", I truly mean it. These are not just words spoken; they have meaning. Other things I have learned about myself are that I enjoy spending time alone, throwing a bag together and traveling whether spontaneous or planned, meeting new people, trying new things that I never had the opportunity to do even if I have to do it alone (I zip-lined for the first-time last year!), preparing healthier foods, spending time with family and friends, I am happiest when I am planning and organizing anything from a small weekend trip, travel nursing jobs and housing (when not for myself, I like to help others) or the business I just opened within three months of it being a mere discussion. It hasn't gone exactly as planned but it's certainly a start and I plan to continue growing it.

10. Setting boundaries. Setting healthy boundaries is a way of taking care of ourselves. I've not done so great with this one as it takes clear and concise communication; and communication is not a strong area for me. I tend to shut down when I feel conflict arising because I don't like to argue. It's a coping mechanism that I haven't truly dealt with yet, but has been fully noted. For some reason, it has been embedded in many of us that paying attention to our own wants and needs is selfish and that is just not true. It is important that during this rat race that we call life, we not only pay attention to our wants and needs, but also have those wants and needs met just as we help others have theirs met. Why is this so difficult for us? These past few years of the COVID-19 pandemic have certainly helped me gain new insight on how

important this is. I am exhausted. So much so that I had to take a step back from bedside nursing. I've worked hard as a nurse over the past almost fifteen years, always feeling like I gave 110% to my job and life while neglecting myself. And relationships. Relationships are supposed to be give and take; they are not to be one-sided. I love people; but I refuse to be the one doing all of the giving. Those are not fulfilling or healthy relationships. Throughout the pandemic I spent a good amount of time alone, reflecting on what I can be better at; and setting boundaries is definitely one of them.

11. Become a business owner. This has been challenging to say the least. I have questioned every decision that I make on a daily basis. I have been excited, nervous and absolutely scared to death from day to day. Through this journey I have learned some new training and skills that will give me new experiences as a family nurse practitioner. Learning new things daily and helping others go hand in hand in the healthcare world and it is something that I am passionate about. I opened this small business with a friend and it just didn't work out as a partnership. I really have been disappointed about this but we live and learn and it's okay because through failure comes success. I am working and growing the business on my own and it has been a learning curve for sure.

12. Take a solo yoga trip to somewhere out of the United States (after I read "Eat, Pray, Love" by Elizabeth Gilbert, I felt that it would be totally necessary to gain my sense of self). The book and the movie had such a profound impact on my life. I know that probably sounds a little silly but for someone that became a mom at twenty years old, a wife at twenty-two, with a

179

full-time job, became a college freshman at twenty-nine and started my first career at thirty-five, I knew that someday I would be this woman; I would be lost, confused, and searching for what I truly desired from this life. I can pinpoint the exact time that I felt this way. This was accomplished in February 2022 and the sole reason that I wrote this chapter. I had intentions of writing a book someday and when this opportunity arose; I was all too ecstatic to take the chance.

13. Writing a book is something that I have aspired to do for many years and I am so excited to be a part of this Women's Warrior Collaboration series! I plan to write a chapter in every single book published in this series. Let me just say that writing this chapter has not been a simple task with so many life responsibilities and starting a new business. There were so many times that I doubted myself and my ability to write this and for days or weeks I was too overwhelmed to open my document to type a single word. I was thrilled and also scared. At times I would let my fear of failure take over. Would my words complete a sentence? Did I know enough of anything to write about? Did I know how to properly structure a sentence? Would it be worthy of reading? I didn't even know what I would write about until I had already written about four pages. Every time I became unmotivated, I thought about the ladies I met on the trip to Costa Rica and how they encouraged and inspired me to do these things that I had been yearning to do for years. And then I would find that fire again...for a short time. Every time I lost my motivation, somehow it would show back up. Our motivation can often be stimulated by our

thoughts, needs, values, and goals. My thoughts were not always on my side, but my needs, values, and goals to be a part of this incredible opportunity are what impelled me to continue. I needed to do this for myself, for my own self-confidence and self-satisfaction. This was important to me because I made this commitment to myself and others and that is important to me. And simply put; it was a goal that I wanted to accomplish. Women need inspiration, encouragement and empowerment and I am elated to have even a small part in this. The day that Jennifer Capella asked me to be a part of this collaboration, it gave me hope of accomplishing a goal that I didn't know if would actually be within my reach. A published author. I'm still not sure I believe I made it this far. This is a wonderful opportunity that wouldn't be happening had I not taken a leap of faith, booked that flight, and went on that solo yoga trip to Costa Rica.

Of course, this is only a short list of goals that I have made for myself over the years. Some are short-term goals while others are long-term goals. There are so many more that I could talk about but I will save you from all of that excessive chatter. Over the years I have written some of my goals down while others remained only in my mind. Dr. Gail Matthews' research data shows that we are 42% more likely to achieve our goals if we write them down or type them out. Writing down our dreams forces us to be specific about what we want and expect to gain from goal setting and goal getting. Visualizing our goals can greatly increase our success as it drives us to take action and track our progress of the goal along the way.

For many years, I wanted to write something. A short story or maybe a book. I never gave any thought on writing a chapter in a book with multiple authors. This has been a challenge but also maybe the coolest thing I have ever done! I have met so many new ladies while writing this book. I look forward to writing more and accomplishing more goals in my next thirty years. On my solo trip, I was inspired to put my hopes and dreams into motion and accomplish some of my goals that seemed a million miles away. Becoming a published author and starting a business were not on my calendar for 2022 or 2023. As a matter of fact, they hadn't even made it to my written down list yet, they were still just thoughts in my mind. They were still waiting to be approved for the five- or ten-year plan and I hadn't decided where to fit them in yet. That all changed very quickly. Things don't always happen in our time; they happen at the right time.

Over the years, I have chatted with several of my patients about writing a book that detailed my travel nursing and life experiences. It seemed more often than not that I formed a bond with the patients I provided nursing care to which led to conversations about our lives. As a nurse, I feel that compassion and empathy, along with building trust improves patient outcomes significantly and that was important to me. Although I have read studies that prove this theory, my experiences are far more convincing.

To this day I still have conversations that I jotted down on scratch paper and cards saved that I received from patients and families so I would not forget them when the day of writing finally came. Many patients gave me their blessing about writing a book and expressed wanting their story to be a part of my story; and they will be. I plan to dedicate an entire chapter on the experiences with patients that I have been so graciously a part of, but in this one I must tell you about one specific experience that will always be special to me. This story makes me cry every time and I am not one who cries often.

In early 2013, John (not his real name) was a patient in the hospital and I was his nurse. I was in John's room giving him pain medication and chatting about life when a doctor burst into room 566 and nonchalantly gave him a *terminal* diagnosis of lung cancer. I remember it like it was yesterday as I just stood there in disbelief. We were having a great conversation about life, when this doctor abruptly interrupted and within 15 seconds, he delivered such devastating news of, "You have lung cancer, it's terminal, no treatments will cure this and all we can offer you is palliative chemotherapy." I just stood there at the foot of John's bed, dismayed and thinking, does this doctor have a clue at how insensitive he sounds delivering this diagnosis the way he did or is he just going through the motions? John just sat there on the side of his bed, all alone. No family, no friends and no support. Only me, his nurse who he had just met a few hours earlier. Now, I do know that doctors do have time constraints and don't always have the ability to wait for family members to rush to the bedside, but as a healthcare professional, I feel that this kind of life altering news should be discussed when the patient's family or support person is available. I think a call ahead to the nurse to have the patient call their family to the bedside is an appropriate action to take before confronting a patient with this kind of shocking information is not too much to ask for. If you are a physician and are reading this, do better. The way some situations are handled in healthcare really blows my mind, but that's a story for another chapter.

I am thankful that I was there that day with John to share in this sorrow. I let him ask questions that he needed answered and when he wanted to know what "palliative chemotherapy" meant, I broke down in tears. I blocked out the beeping of my pager (yes, an old school pager) that was constantly going off on my hip, while I just sat with him and allowed him time to process his new reality. All that John knew was that his mother and father had both died of cancer as he was their caregiver throughout their battle with chemo and radiation and he wanted no part of that. The conversations that I had with him over those three shifts changed my life forever, for the better. I just wish that somehow, I could have changed his life course at that moment. My patient with a terminal diagnosis of cancer was helping me to see through life a little more clearly while his life was coming to an end.

He was sixty-two years old with so much life still left to live and yet there was nothing that could give him the time that he wanted. I believe in God and I know that we don't get to choose our time; but these are by far the most difficult times for me as a nurse. Over the years I've had more of these times than I care to admit. Cancer does not discriminate, it is vicious, and I will never understand how we haven't found a cure for it, but we put a man on the moon in 1969. According to my research, too much money is wasted on flawed and unsubstantiated studies and we should be using as much funding as we can to find a cure for cancer. Of course, that's just my opinion.

John didn't just encourage me to pursue my dream of travel nursing; he told me the story of how he planned to travel the world someday once his military years were up, and for him that day never came. He talked of how he saved all of his money while in the military, eating in the mess hall for most meals and not splurging on going out when all of his buddies did. He served his country for more than twenty years. He was deployed and fought in wars, but the cruelest war he would fight was not with military issued weapons, but against toxic cells inside his body. His war was just beginning. He had sacrificed so much with the intentions of enjoying his life after his retirement in his early fifties. But that didn't happen for him. After his retirement, John's mother was first diagnosed with cancer and then several years later his father was diagnosed with cancer. He spent the first part of retirement as their caregiver. Once they both passed, money was tight from all of the medical expenses and most of his savings was gone. I remember the words John said to me on my third shift of being his nurse. I went into his room after I had given the report to the oncoming nurse to tell him goodbye and that I would be praying for him and he touched my hand and said, "young lady, please don't wait until you think the time is right to travel, do it now. If it is something that you truly want to experience and you can find a way, do it." His words were powerful and they opened my eyes. I didn't want to leave him that day. I have always been the nurse that didn't like leaving my patients knowing that it would probably be the last time I ever spoke to them.

Although I always enjoyed traveling, I rarely ventured outside of the little town that I was from and had lived for the greatest part of my life. After three shifts of intense conversations with John, I decided it was time to take the chance and leap into the unknown world of travel nursing. At this point in my life my marriage had fallen apart, my daughter had graduated high school and it was time for me to do something for ME. In August of 2013, I took my very first travel nurse contract in Tulsa, Oklahoma (not where I wanted but I was new at this and it was just the beginning-more about this to come later in the series). I had never been away from my family for more than a few days in my entire life but I found myself driving West to Tulsa, Oklahoma to start a new journey.

Thank goodness I wasn't totally alone in this as I convinced my friend Heather that she also needed to experience the unknown...and the fun of course. I left my first nursing job where I had amazing co-workers and a well-managed unit (which I have found is a rarity) to work a contract from hell. I'm sure if hell was a place on earth, this was it. It was by far one of the two worst contracts out of the twenty that I've worked over the last nine years. It was terrifying, shocking, and an eye-opener to see how differently hospitals operated just four states apart. The Oklahoma contract proved to be a real challenge, though Tulsa itself was a fun experience. Just to give you a small blip of what it felt like, Heather and I would listen to DMX- "Party Up" on the way to work just to get motivated for what the night was about to throw at us. Difficult and stressful is an understatement to describe the duties this hospital and management expected of its nurses. Heather and I left Oklahoma the morning after our last shift so fast I don't even remember packing our cars. We couldn't wait to get back home and work where we felt it was a safe environment for nursing and our patients.

That first contract put patient safety into perspective for me. It taught me that I better know what I'm doing because in this new world of travel nursing; I was on my own. The things that I could talk about from those few months in that hospital still have me wondering about many things ten years later. Thank you, John, for encouraging me to get out into the world to chase my dreams; without your encouragement I may have never known just how bad a hospital could treat their staff. Although, it may have been the hardest contract of all my years in travel nursing; it was a learning experience that didn't break me, but prepared me to find contracts that better suited me over the next nine years. Thank goodness I didn't allow that one bad experience to dictate my future in travel nursing or end my travel nursing career; I gave it eight more years and every new city was an adventure that I will never forget! I don't have one single regret from this career path. It has been rewarding and fulfilling in many ways.

Flash forward seven years to the Spring of 2020 and the COVID-19 pandemic is exploding around the world. I have been a nurse for twelve years and a travel nurse for seven of those. I just graduated with my Master's degree in Nursing with a specialization as a Family Nurse Practitioner and was organizing a study plan to become board certified and advance my career path from a bedside nurse to a nurse practitioner. I was excited and ready for this new change. We, as healthcare workers, had no idea what we would be faced with in the hospital setting. We have ALL been affected by this global pandemic in one way or another and for healthcare workers, the pandemic affected us from every single direction. As a registered nurse who worked in cities where the pandemic hit hard, such as New York City and Phoenix; I saw how patients, families, business owners, workforces, healthcare workers and all Americans were affected; not just daily, but second by second. Everyone has their own tragedies and stories to tell, and this is a little about mine.

In mid-January of 2020 after completing my degree, I was ready for a much-needed brain break. It had taken me from February 2017 until January 2020 to complete this program while living somewhat of a roller coaster of a lifestyle. I was mentally exhausted and burned out with what felt like a sauteed cerveau (better known as fried brain). Information overload is when the information available exceeds the processing abilities of the individual in the time available. This meant that my brain could not possibly produce anything else productive at this point until it had a HARD RESET. So, what did I do? I booked a flight on January 10th and headed to New York City to relax, reset my brain and spend some time with my cousins.

Who would've known that in less than a week into my brain reset, all news outlets would be covering details about a virus that could possibly spread like wildfire and kill who knows how many people. While sitting on the sofa in my family's apartment in the upper East Side of NYC, we watched multiple news media outlets discussing the timeline unfolding and telling of the discovery of this Wuhan, China virus. On January 20, 2020 the Centers for Disease Control and Prevention announced that three United States airports would start screening passengers coming into the country and on January 21, 2020 the first case of coronavirus was confirmed in Washington state. It was at that moment that I knew it was time for me to end my vacation and book a flight back home to South Carolina. We all can google search and see that in 2020, NYC had a population of over eight million people with a land mass of a little over 300 square miles and is the most densely populated city in the United States; meaning a lot of people in a little bit of space which was somewhere that most would not want to be when a catastrophic event occurred. I happen to be from a very small town that has a population of about twenty-seven thousand in the entire county, with a land mass of 516 square miles; a very different geographical setting and population. It was just a matter of time that this virus spread to every major densely populated city in the United States and it was an unsettling thought. Little did we know that soon COVID-19 would be in every neighborhood, town and city, killing more than one million in the United States.

Although I had always wanted to contribute by working in some form of natural disaster relief and a mission trip, working during a pandemic was something that had never crossed my mind; but as a nurse I felt called to do whatever I could to help those in need. Becoming a nurse changed me in so many ways and I feel like it was one of two great accomplishments for me; the other being a mom. Having an impact on the lives of others is why I became a nurse. My patients would often tell me that I was doing what I was called to do and they could see it in how I cared for them. Since I always wanted to contribute my skills and experience as a nurse to working disaster relief or a mission trip and had not yet been able to, it only made sense that I go to the place with the greatest need for nurses at that moment, which was NYC. Not many could understand why I felt compelled to put myself in the middle of the unknown or thought I was being selfish; it was not a difficult decision for me. I wanted to go to NYC and offer my support in any way that I could. I am a believer that when we feel the call to do something, that call will enable us to use our skills, experiences, and gifts and it will align with our beliefs and values. And for me, this just made sense. Becoming a nurse gave me a sense of self-confidence, self-esteem and a purpose that I had never had before. And for me this calling to NYC had purpose.

In April of 2020, I found a contract in NYC, packed my bags, and flew back into the busiest city in the United States; except this time, you could hear a pin drop in the LaGuardia Airport. On a usual day, the streets would be overcrowded with people rushing through their daily routine of lights, crosswalks, catching the train to wherever they may be going, and horns obnoxiously honking. Not this time, this time I was apprehensive by the eerie silence. I felt like I was in a movie where at any moment something would appear from the sky and attack the city. It was that bizarre. The few people that were outside on the street were quiet and seemed afraid that talking might spread the virus through their masks. And so was I. We were truthfully in the midst of the unknown.

I will never forget that day; or so many other days during those ten weeks of working in NYC. The cab ride from the airport to the hotel wearing a face mask in complete silence. Walking the city streets to search for somewhere that was open to buy food. Walking into the Grand Central terminal and being one of two people on the subway car that would usually be so full you could barely stand. I was in a place that I had just been two months prior and it seemed like a different world.

On my first day in the hospital, I was told that lunch breaks were mandatory and I was made to take one. What? Take a lunch break? In the middle of a pandemic? I rarely had a lunch break throughout my entire nursing career and now during a pandemic I was getting a lunch break. All I could think was that I have all this new charting, how to page doctors, and new equipment to learn and I don't have time to eat. But since it was mandatory, I took my lunch break and sat in silence in a cafeteria with my mask on. Since it only took me about ten minutes to devour my lunch, I decided to take a walk outside and around the block to get some fresh air. At first, I didn't realize what I was seeing as it was unexpected. I just stood there staring for a few moments. Seeing two freezer trucks parked outside of the hospital was truly the moment that I understood the magnification of what was going on around me. What was going on all over the world. New York City was quiet and still with only a few cars on the street. No horns honking angrily. No people hurrying to cross the street in a crowd. No one in Grand Central Station; and I mean no one. I have pictures to prove it. We were on lockdown. LOCKDOWN. People were afraid for their lives. I was afraid for my own. Although the streets were calm, the hospital was overwhelmed on a level that is hard to describe. Sort of similar to a small-scale war zone. This was only my sixth day in NYC for this job and I was nervous about what was to come. Every twelve-hour day in the hospital was filled with an unending cacophony of heart monitors, bipap machines, IV pumps, call lights and code blue calls overhead every few minutes. Used gowns, masks, and face shields overflowed the trash cans and littered the hallways. It was a constant state of frenzy with sheer panic in the eyes of staff and patients. In the first few weeks of being there my nights were sleepless because my brain just couldn't stop hearing all of the alarms and cries for help. Sirens were all over the city throughout the night making it hard to fall asleep even after a long day of work. There were other healthcare workers staying in the hotel where I was and sometimes at night, we would sit around and talk about what we had encountered throughout our day. Too tired to listen but too stressed to sleep, talking through it with others got us all through the daily roller coaster we got on at six am and didn't get off of until eight pm. Just like-minded people sharing their thoughts, feelings, and emotional burdens about what was going on in the world around us. It was like an emotional support group meeting but unintentional.

I spent ten weeks in NYC in a hotel, eating out of a mini refrigerator in my room, sending my clothes to be laundered, taking the subway to and from the hospital, being a caregiver for the sickest patients that I have ever cared for, holding the hands of dying patients because they were alone, spending most of my time working, in bed exhausted, or soaking up some sun on a park bench just listening to the chatter of birds; and yet I still know that I was exactly where I was meant to be. After my ten weeks in NYC, I flew home, spent a little time recovering and then flew to Phoenix, Arizona to work as a crisis nurse in another COVID-19 hot spot. This was not the first time I had worked in Phoenix as a travel nurse and it just felt like the right thing for me to do. During this time, Phoenix had the highest rate of positive COVID-19 tests of any place in the World. But unlike NYC, Phoenix wasn't shut down and the people weren't hoarded up in their homes afraid. People were out living their lives. It was sort of an odd feeling after leaving NYC. I remember thinking how it felt like it was two completely different worlds although so many people were dying in both places. After Phoenix, I traveled to the island of Guam, where I worked for six months. This was another drastic change. Because they have a population of less than 200,000 people, they were dedicated to keeping people alive. It was a community of caring, love, and compassion. For this job I had to be interviewed and deemed competent to even be considered for the contract. The company I worked for wanted to know that I would be able to handle working in conditions that may not be what I was accustomed to. The hospitals in Guam weren't equipped like we were used to. Walking up to the hospital on my first day was exhilarating. There I was on an island almost 8,000 miles from home and I was excited to be there doing something I had never thought I would have the opportunity to do. At this point I had already been caring for covid patients for almost a year and I felt like I could handle that part of the job. I wasn't sure about the idea of working in a facility where I wouldn't have access to many of the basic necessities that I am used to having readily available and although I felt culturally competent, I wasn't sure if I would be able to properly communicate so that I could give the care that the patients needed. Let me say this, it was by far the best nursing job I have ever worked, with the best people I have ever had the pleasure of working with, and the best patients I have ever cared for. I could have lived among these people forever if I could have convinced my family to move. They were a blessing to me and showed me what it meant to be a part of a community that cared for its people. After six months, I had to leave the amazing little island of Guam, but it and its people will forever have a special place in my heart.

After Guam, I went back to Phoenix for one more round until I just couldn't do it anymore. In February 2022, I was standing in the hallway on unit 1B to the point of tears, not sure which patient to run to first, when the words "When is enough enough?" popped into my mind. Those words will forever echo in my mind. I was working on a unit that was understaffed with two nurses, one nursing assistant and fourteen practically bedridden patients; most of which had immediate needs. I have always taken the role of being a nurse and patient advocate seriously and I was tired of being treated as though I was another warm body by corporations, administration, and management. Patients deserve better. Nurses and nursing aides deserve better. Families deserve better. I have given so much of myself to the profession throughout the past years as a nurse and it was simple at that very moment; enough was enough. I completed my contract one week later, packed all six of my overweight suitcases, and boarded a plane headed back east to South Carolina. I do not tell you all of this to gain sympathy. Every experience that I had during my nursing career has had a profound effect on my life in one way or another. Nursing will always be my career, it's just time to move into a different direction.

I am grateful that during the pandemic I was able to contribute what God has so graciously gifted me with; compassion and empathy. Our communities and families have all been touched by the pandemic in one way or another. It changed us as a country and I am not sure that we will ever fully recover as individuals, communities, or a nation. I have not returned to a hospital to work as a nurse practitioner as I have started my own small business in which I hope to grow while I also work part-time for a company making house calls where I don't hear the incessant sounds of alarms and beeping while working understaffed. Even though I have not worked as a bedside nurse since February 2022, when I hear any of my appliances at home or anything in my car start beeping, I am extremely irritated by them and maybe even a little traumatized.

Nothing has happened in my life that was not supposed to happen. My life is on the exact path that it was meant for. At times, we must make directional changes so that we can continue challenging ourselves to be the best version of ourselves that we can be. It all depends on your goals and what you want to achieve from them. Although I have achieved many of the goals that I have set for myself already, I still have many more to come. I will always be thinking about what is next? I accomplished writing this chapter even though it turned out nothing like what I had expected but I just went with it.

I was forty-eight years old when I came to the realization that although life is not perfect, our individual story is perfect and unique in our own way. None of what I have told you about in this chapter would be possible without the other. These goals tell the story of my life. Thank you, Jennifer; for believing in me and inviting me to be a part of this book. Ladies around the world, we can accomplish anything that we set our mind to. Please don't let fear or failure keep you from the success that awaits you! As the title of this book says, "Never Fear Your Fire." Face it, challenge it, and walk through the damn fire; victory awaits you on the other side! Cheers to new goals, new beginnings, women encouraging women, and many more chapters to come in the Women Warrior Collaboration series.

My name is Wendy Murphy Knox. I am a Family Nurse Practitioner and a new small business owner to an Aesthetic, Health and Wellness practice. I have worked in healthcare for 26 years, 14 of those years have been as a registered nurse and now nurse practitioner. I started my career in the healthcare system in a temporary position in the billing department in 1997, continuing on as a receptionist in 2005, a patient care tech in 2007, a licensed practical nurse in 2008, a registered nurse in 2008, received my Bachelor of Science in Nursing in 2012, and completed my Master's of Science in Nursing degree in 2020. I then pursed my dream of becoming a board-certified Family Nurse Practitioner in 2020. I have traveled across the United States as a travel nurse to 15 hospitals over the last nine years with the beautiful island of Guam being the farthest from home. I have set many goals for myself throughout my life personally and professionally, and continue to achieve each of them. After becoming a mom to my only daughter Kayla 28 years ago, she inspired me to become the best mother, person and woman that I could be; for myself and for others. I am proud to say that she is also a nurse. Becoming a nurse taught me to have empathy and compassion for others, with both being an invaluable asset to patient care and improving patient outcomes. I am truly passionate in being a patient advocate and educating myself as much as I can to benefit everyone that I provide care to. Making even the smallest difference is better than making no difference at all. Year forty-eight of my life proved to be a year that I discovered that life indeed is meant to be lived to its fullest potential and that we are solely responsible to make that happen for ourself through self-care, self-discovery, and self-love. Confront your fears and use them to your benefit; for fear can be a powerful motivator.

First, I would like to thank Jennifer Capella for the opportunity to write this chapter and the many other chapters to come. If I hadn't taken that solo vacation to Costa Rica we would've never met or discussed our hopes and dreams. You motivated me to work towards my dreams. Secondly, I would like to thank my mother. You are the most resilient, hard-working woman I know. I am forever grateful for everything you taught me as I would not be where I am today without you. I admire and love you. Lastly, thank you to my beautiful daughter, Kayla. Being your mom challenged me in many ways; like riding roller coasters with you just so you wouldn't be afraid of them like I was. And I first learned that I enjoy writing as I was helping you learn to write book reports ;). You inspired me to be the best version of me and the bond we share will always be. I love you to the moon and back.

Chapter 13:
Don't Let Your Mind, Bully Your Body

Analexa Rivera

We live in a society where when you look at someone thin, you would think they have the ideal figure. You wouldn't understand the depression that could come with a thin figure and how it could affect a person so badly. Well, let me tell you one thing; it absolutely DOES! I always remind myself of these words "think before you speak" and I believe it truly could change people's perspective on another person if they did this act. Until now, I have struggled to find the words to paint the picture of pure skinny-shaming and how WORDS can run deep to someone. Adults and children should learn that skinny-shaming is part of bullying as well. My name is Analexa Rivera. Original sinner. Rebellious Woman. The Flakita in the family. My story is about finding the beauty in me. The proudest me and the acceptance of my body. Myself.

I grew up mostly all of my life in Jersey City, NJ with separated parents. My parents separated when I was one and a half years old. I didn't see any arguments growing up between them but I did know there was some hatred between them. Ever just see two people around each other and you could feel the tension between them but they aren't saying anything? That's how it was between my parents. I know they didn't really like each other but they always wanted to show that they could still co-parent for the sake of me. I never knew the full true story of what happened between them because I always got two different sides. I had two older brothers but we had different fathers, I never considered them my half-brothers since I was always around them. My mom never got married when I was younger but my father did. He met someone when I was two years old and she is now my step-mother. Having a second mom was a blessing in disguise. She treated me with love and respect as if I was her own child. My step-mother became pregnant when I was 12 years ago and I instantly knew I would have a baby sister. I knew that God gave my step-mother a girl because he saw how she raised me as her own. Throughout my childhood, I did wonder what it would be like if my parents were together. I know things happen for a reason and this is how life should be; but I always did wonder. In school, mostly all of my friends had parents who were together. People could view from the outside on how I could be this happy child with more love than I could imagine but nobody truly knows how you deeply feel. I hated the back and forth with my parents and having to pack my bags each time. I always wanted to be at one place more when I was already there. I never wanted to leave. It sucked each time doing that. I know it was for the best and I was always around great family members. I just hated the process of it all. The times that I couldn't do what I wanted to do and one parent allowed it, it gave me anxiety at times and just made me lash out in anger. The attitude started coming in and I wanted to be this rebellious child. Growing up with my mom also knowing I have another mom in my life at a young age wasn't easy either. My mom always wanted me to be happy and none of my parents knew that words could really run deep to a person. I did have the opinions of my step-mother in my ear but I know it must have been hard on her. I just never understood why my mom didn't really like my step mom at first. I just knew that she was my mom and now I have a step-mom. I knew I loved them both equally and my step-mother showed me the same love my mom did. I had an accident when I was around six years old when I was outside with my brother's friend's little brother playing with the skateboard. My mother was inside at the time and had my brother responsible of me. While playing with the skateboard, I decided to skateboard with my eyes closed and I ended up busting my face in a tree with a beer bottle on the floor and planted my face right on it. My whole face had scratches and my two front teeth were completely damaged. I remember my mom coming outside and bringing me in to clean me up. A few days later, my mother took me to my father's house but never notified him of what happened to me that day. My father was highly upset that he didn't receive a call from her that same exact day it happened. Those were the times that I understood why my father would get angry with my mother. I also knew that my mother did the very best she could. She was a single parent with three kids and having my father in my life was helpful but I know it must have been tough to raise two boys on her own. My brothers are her world and there were times that I felt like she forgot she also had a daughter. She would do everything for me but felt like she would always go above and beyond for them. My family always provided me with that love but I still had this huge void in my life. My dad had a different point of view than my mother. Parenting skills were a bit different with each other. My dad was more on the strict side and my mother gave me a bit more freedom. Throughout my childhood, I always wanted to be super independent. I have always endeavored to get everything on my own without needing to ask for help from my parents. While I attended catholic school for most of my grammar school years, I had a love-hate relationship with the institution. While I loved the school, having friends who did things that I wanted to do was often a source of frustration for me. Boys from my school would constantly tell me that I'm skinny and I need to gain weight. When a person tells you that if you gain a few more pounds, you would look perfect, that isn't a compliment. It's pretty insulting since clearly you're stating that I'm not perfect the way I am right now.

I grew up with mostly boys around me because I had my older brothers. I was a bit of a tom-boy growing up and grew up pretty tough. In catholic school, my group of friends would always get their hair done or nails done. They would shave their arms and legs already. We had to wear our uniform dress or skirt for school but I would always roll up my skirt to make it shorter. I was this rebellious child that wanted to do everything that I wanted to do and not listen to my parents. I would roll it up once they dropped me off and pull it back down when they picked me up. I felt ugly with that long dress and every other girl was doing the same thing, so why not me? My father on the other hand didn't approve of me doing this whatsoever and caught me with my skirt too short one day. He didn't understand that I just liked it better when it was shorter. I wanted to fit in with everyone else when I was younger and have everyone like me. I was easy to get along with and I always wanted to do what everyone else was doing. I remember when I saw my friend dye her hair so I wanted streaks of blonde in my hair. I knew if I asked my father, I wouldn't have been able to get it done, so I asked my mother. My mom told me yes and she did it for me. She only did two streaks of blonde in my hair at the front. I knew I was going to get in trouble with my dad but it was frustrating to me because my mother always said yes and not to worry about it. She would basically just take the blame for me. The next week, I went to my dad's house with two streaks of blonde hair and I immediately got in trouble. My father kept repeatedly telling me that I was too young to do that to my hair and that I would damage my hair. I had to sit at the dining room table and write "I will never dye my hair again" about 100 times. I hated the punishment with a passion. I felt like it was the end of the world. I understood my dad didn't want that done, but it would anger me that my mom allowed things that my father didn't. It just put so much heaviness on me because I didn't know who to really listen to. I know my mother just wanted whatever made her daughter happy, but was it the right parenting? Was my father just being too harsh? It was such a battle to me and I don't think they fully saw how it affected me. When the girls did shave their legs in school, I would use nair to remove the hair. I hated that I had to do the opposite of what other people were doing. I didn't understand that I was young and didn't need to worry about hair on my body. It made me feel ugly at times because I knew I was hairier than everyone else. I remember walking to gym one day in grammar school and one boy from my school said "Ew you have long hair on your arms". I felt embarrassed and never wanted hair on my arm again. I hated that the boys in my school always noticed everything on a girl and would pick on the little things. People would constantly ask me "when are you going to shave your unibrow" and I would always just say "people have hair on their bodies". I hated getting those ridiculous comments people would say even though they didn't think they were being offensive. Often times, I think people don't intend to harm someone's feelings but in reality, it always does. Nobody likes to hear something they don't like about themselves, especially consistently. My father would always say "Boys that pick on girls, that means they like them." I understand that but they shouldn't do it at all. Those little comments really made me feel depressed at times and want to just run away from it all. Even though I didn't grow up in a crazy home with abusive parents or substance abuse, I still wasn't a happy child. I wanted to be an adult already so badly. I remember telling my dad that I couldn't wait to get older. I didn't want to deal with the whole rules and discipline. My mother allowed me to go to friend's houses and sleepover so I would often want to just stay with my mom. The more freedom she gave me, the more I wanted to just stay at my mom's. I loved being at my dad's but I hated the strictness. Even though my mother did have a boyfriend, I know she was always alone so I liked being with her. The times I saw my mother argue with her boyfriend, I hated seeing my mom go through that. I would always have my mother's back and always went next to her if she did get in an argument with a boyfriend. I knew if I was by her, nobody would harm her. I always had a great relationship with my mother. As you get older, you realize that having that strict household is for the better. It's about discipline, tough love and making sure you go down the right path. Parents just want you to be better than they were. My father always wanted me to succeed in life and be happy. He provided me with everything and never left my side. My father could've left me back when I was young and just left my mom with three kids, but he never did. He put me in a good school, made sure I had clothes on my back, put me in activities and sports, and overall gave me a great childhood. People frankly thought I always had it all because I had parents that loved me, but I had this ideal life in my head. I want to be independent and I want to be an adult. I didn't want to listen to any rules by anyone and I wanted to live it on my terms. I always yearned to dress more seductively because I hated how I looked. Being skinny didn't always make me feel so beautiful so I would like to show off a bit of my skin.

I was an athletic girl in grammar school and in high school, I stayed playing basketball. I was mostly happy when I did play ball and it kept my grades up. You get a sense of discipline with sports and I truly believe that it starts involving in all aspects of your life. The only thing that kept me down was people constantly telling me I should eat or pick out my flaws. I have a pretty defined jaw but everybody thought it was too big for my face. My brother's friends would constantly call me "Jaws" when they asked for me or sing the music that plays in the background of the movie. At that time, I'm young and didn't want anything to really bother me. I didn't want anyone to see that it did affect me and it did hurt my feelings. I would constantly look in the mirror and ask "why does my jaw have to be this big?" I know boys liked to pick on girls but I think boys picking on girls are the worst. During that time, I started to think boys were cute and having crushes but how could I get a crush if people constantly think this of me. I would constantly ask myself "Would anyone think I'm pretty with a unibrow and big jaw like this? Would anyone want to date a skinny girl like me? I've had friends and total strangers ask me if I'm anorexic and I wouldn't think that they were trying to offend me in any way but it's like they say "think before you speak". People didn't see how they could offend someone and I would hate that specific word due to the fact that people do go through that. It's not a light word to just use around like it's nothing. I told my friend one time when they did ask me that, "How about if I was? Don't you see that it could really hurt someone's feelings." The amount of times that I got depressed was because of how I looked and my weight. Getting called "chicken legs" or saying I'm shaped like a pancake, put me in a state of mind that I didn't even want to be here anymore. A lot of the girls in my school already had full grown breasts and had a thick figure to them.

I easily made friends with people at my school but there was one time when a friend said "you know if you gained a few pounds and looked slim-thick, you would be perfect" and I just smiled and laughed. I didn't know how to respond to that without getting into an argument with someone. How does a person not think that's insulting? So I'm not perfect the way I look right now, is that what you're telling me? I would never in a million years tell someone that they look fat, so why is it acceptable for someone to say they look too skinny. People think it's a compliment to say that to someone but then it's wrong if you comment on someone's overweight figure. Being skinny isn't as good as it seems and just like people that are overweight, it could come with issues that you don't want. The desire to gain weight and trying to fit in clothes that could give you some type of figure was excruciating. I did want to gain a few pounds, I always wanted to be a little thicker than I was but I couldn't. It's not like I didn't eat a lot because I always did, I just had a fast metabolism. I don't think people realize how harmful it is to say to someone that they are skinny because it surely is skinny-shaming. I don't care what anyone else calls it, it's skinny-shaming. I grew up looking at magazines and always noticing how the models were skinny. People portrayed being skinny like it was the ideal figure to be and you should be happy to be the weight that you are. Walking in the streets wasn't always with people looking at you as if you were pretty, you would get those disapproving glances. I would get strangers coming to me and telling me " you're so skinny" and it's like " I know, I know I am skinny". Even while I was eating, people would say " you eat like a bird" and it would just sicken me that people are so worried about what other people do. Many people think being skinny and pretty would bring you happiness but that's not true. I think often times it's even worse because you see yourself as this beautiful girl but deep down, you truly don't think you are. All of my life I've been told how skinny I was and it broke me more and more once people I loved and trusted told me I was. It was like a smack in the face. Having relations with boys was quite hard because sometimes, arguments would lead to body-shaming and I never could look at someone the same after. How could I surround myself with someone that thinks I'm too skinny and I need to get thick.

This is just how I look and that's how God made me. Everyone should be happy with the way God made them. You're unique in your own way. It mentally affected me for a while but once I graduated high school, I started to notice that once I shifted my negative responses to myself about "why am I so skinny", I started to just embrace my figure. I realized that people started getting surgeries done and getting more defined jaw lines like mine. Being young, you feel like you should care so much about how you look but you shouldn't at all. You should just live your young years and enjoy being a child. When I look back at my childhood, I realized that I had loving parents and even though my dad was as strict on me, I'm truly grateful for that. Having those types of parents are rare and everyone should appreciate it. You don't want a parent that doesn't care at all what you do and just lets you ruin your life. You want someone by your side through it all and teaching you a better way of life than they had. To the people that repeatedly told me I was skinny and I should gain more weight, thank you for making me embrace my beauty inside and out. Thank you for letting me be a voice for all my skinny people that don't feel heard. I'm here with you and make your journey beautiful as it could be. Create a space to love yourself, outside of what you want other people to love about you. People won't always like you and accept you but the importance of reminding yourself that you are beautiful in your own way will come a long way. This is why I created a clothing/accessory line called "LeAlpha Collection" which is trendy motivational quotes and Alpha Male/Female designed clothing with accessories. I want everyone to feel like an alpha in their own way and own their self-confidence. This shows who I am as a woman and I'm embracing the confidence in my skin. I'm a Woman Warrior that never lets anyone's opinion define me and always walk with grace.

Tips on what not to say to others about their thin figure

- You're so skinny- We already know that. You don't have to say it.
- You're all skin and bones
- You look anorexic
- You should eat more, you are too skinny
- Why are you so skinny
- You need to have more meat on your bones
- Chicken legs
- Pancake

Analexa Rivera is a multi-talented individual originally from Jersey City, New Jersey and residing in Bayonne, NJ. Currently, she works as an Assistant Manager for a liquor store where she focuses on developing her sales and entrepreneurial skills. She has spent the majority of her career in the customer service industry, gaining experiences in areas such as problem solving, sales, and marketing. After earning her certifications in Meta Social Media Marketing and Bookkeeping basics, she entered the entrepreneur world to explore her passion in designing apparels and accessories. She focuses on investing in stocks and enhancing her skills for future success. While working on her brand, she also enjoys hiking, visiting antique shops, spending time with her family, and most importantly spending time with her dog. Analexa is setting a new standard for how to be confident, fearless, and embracing your beauty. Embrace what God has given you and never let others' opinions define you. She is honored to be a member of Woman's Warriors Collab which is a group of women that promote women's sense of self-worth and share knowledge and experiences. Analexa participates in political campaigns in both Jersey City and Bayonne as a volunteer. Analexa has added philanthropy to her continued success story, supporting the less fortunate through year-round food and blood drives, toy drives for children, and even raising funds for animal charities. She also aims to improve the lives of animals by donating to American Humane. One of her aspirations is to travel the world and aid animals in different countries.

Website www.lealphacollection.com
IG:@xmisslexax
TikTok: @_missalpha_
Facebook: Analexa Rivera

I would like to thank both of my parents Millie and David. I'm eternally grateful for the discipline, support, & loving me through all the obstacles in my life. To my step-mother Lily, Thank you for always guiding me to the right path. Each one of you have shaped me to be the strong woman I am today.

Chapter 14
When Life Gives You Lemons, It's Time to Make Lemonade

Jeanette Diaz

E verything that happens is perfect, just, and necessary. I have come to terms and realize that statement could not be more accurate. I now look at life through that lens and it has made a world of difference. What isn't a lesson is a blessing. I am the woman I am today because of the experiences that have shaped me. I have learned and grown as a result and wouldn't change it. Changing my past would change the essence of the core of who I am as a human being.

As a child you live carefree not realizing that those are some of the best years of your life. During those years experiences we live have a deep impact and mark us in ways that as an adult it takes years to unravel and get to the root of why we are the way we are. I had a great childhood. My parents provided what was within their means, resources, and education. I grew up surrounded by family and friends who loved me and only wanted the best for me. I have a big family on both sides. Growing up my cousins were my friends. In every family no matter how big or small there are always challenges. Because of these challenges it doesn't mean we will see eye to eye. We all know this to be true for our very own families. I've healed my inner child and as a result now know that every decision and experience my parents made was out of love and necessity.

I was very young when I started my family. I was hopeful that my relationship would be a lifelong one.

Which is why I continued ignoring the red flags thinking, hoping, and wishing things would change. Things got better temporarily but not for long. The realization that it was a relationship where the other person wanted full control made the decision of ending it easier but not faster. It took six long years. I look back and think, Why did I stay so long? Why didn't I muster the courage to go? How could I be so naïve? I knew it was bad and only getting worse. I needed to reach the point of saturation. I needed to know that as bad as it was leaving was better any day of the week than staying. The only person who could decide was me. I didn't want my daughters being raised thinking this type of relationship is healthy, normal, or acceptable. This decision was a very difficult one for me even though deep down inside I knew it was the only one. I was constantly told "who's going to want a woman with kids?", "You are damaged goods and will be alone for the rest of your life." These statements were far from the truth. Those are the statements of a person who wants to control you and make you think there are no other options except to remain.

Leaving was the most liberating decision I ever made. I felt as if a heavy weight was lifted off my shoulders. Even though there were a lot of unknowns, I was willing to face those knowing that I didn't need to be in an abusive, manipulative, controlling relationship. What was ironic for me was that family members that knew what was going on wondered why I decided to call it quits. How could these "family members" think that it was healthy or acceptable for me to stay and continue exposing my daughters to that. My response was if I was your daughter or sister what advice would you give me. Not expecting that response from me I gave them the wow factor. Most were at a loss for words. Once I ended the relationship, I was told by my family and friends we didn't know you had a voice. You drowned your identity in your relationship. One thing is to dedicate yourself to your relationship and children and the other is to forget who you are. Before being a wife or mother, you are a human, woman, daughter, sister, cousin, and friend. These are all roles that you had prior to you procreating. These roles don't cease to exist because you have your own immediate family. This is an experience I don't want anyone to go through. I know this is the story of many women and men who think that there is no hope. I'm here to tell you that you can rewrite your story and have that happy ending you have always dreamed of. This doesn't mean that you will not have hardships or struggles. We were all created to be happy and it's what we all long for.

That experience helped me learn the following; nothing is forever, no one can love you unless you love yourself first, things that are worth it take time, there is no need to rush it, your voice and you matter, if something doesn't feel right then it isn't, and never ignore the red flags.

I'm here to tell you with my experience that nothing of what I was told came to fruition.

I used my experience to help me catapult to new experiences and destinations. That was my driving force.

Being a single parent is no joke. You are the good and the bad cop. I take my hat off to all single parents, it takes a village. I am grateful, thankful, and blessed that my village had my back while I was raising my daughters and continue to have my back.

I don't want you to think that life is not full of many highs and lows. I have had many good and bad experiences. I have taken the things that serve me and left what hasn't.

I've raised two beautiful daughters on my own. They turned out to be good young adults, they are both college graduates. We've had our ups and downs. They both know that I am their number one fan and their hardest critic all in one. I have shown them with my example and not my word that life isn't easy and when you get lemons it's time to make lemonade.

I managed to get my honors bachelor's degree full time at night in four years while working a full-time job and being a single parent. Whatever you put your mind to with the right determination you will achieve it. Having my daughters in the audience at the graduation while walking across the stage was truly an honor I would never forget. It was a proud moment having them see me achieve that milestone.

Traveling is one of my passions. I've been fortunate to have traveled to over 20 different countries. I enjoy traveling because there is so much you learn from other cultures and history. You get to see how other people live and their vast traditions. It's amazing to see when you visit other countries that the people who have the least, live the happiest. Yet we have so much and are always striving for more because what we have is not enough. The world is very big, and I can't wait to see where my travel adventures will bring me next.

I never thought I would be a homeowner and it became a reality. With the help of family and friends I was able to achieve the American dream. This has opened the doors to build generational wealth and serves as a measure of financial security. It opens the doors for many other real estate's purchases my family and I will make.

After 22 years God blessed me with my little ray of son- shine. Enzo has been pure joy, happiness and blessings for our household. Starting all over is not easy however, when you are starting again with experience and a partner by your side it makes it all worthwhile. Embarking on pregnancy and parenthood again has been rewarding. I must take my hat off and thank John for being my better half and the father our household needed. It has been quite the ride and we are here for it. I was growing up while I was raising my daughters and now with my son it's different because I am not alone, and I am able to soak it all in.

Sharing your story is never easy, where do I start and how much do I share. I know that my story and words have an impact and will make a difference for someone. Your story will be someone else's survival guide. I exhort you to continue sharing your story because people are listening and if you can change the life of one person you have made a difference.

Life is a roller coaster, and it has its ups and downs. Many doors have closed and so many others have opened. Along with the doors that have opened the breadth of knowledge, influence and network of the people I have connected with is extraordinary. I'm excited at what the future holds in terms of dreams, goals, business plans and everything else in between. I want to leave a legacy for the world and my family that will continue to live long after I have transcended.

Jeanette Diaz, popularly known as JD, is a highly accomplished C-Level Suite Senior Executive Assistant, businesswoman, and author of a chapter in the upcoming best-selling book, Never Fear Your Fire. She is a proud member of Women's Warrior, a group of powerful women sharing their stories of survival, grit, and empowerment in the same book. With over 28 years of experience, JD has honed her travel, volunteer work, and customer service skills, becoming a seasoned professional in her field.

JD is a second-generation Dominican American, born and raised in Brooklyn, NY, and currently residing in New Jersey with her better half of 14 years, John. She is a proud mother of three, with two daughters, Janiece and Ashley, and a young son, Enzo. JD graduated with honors, earning her Bachelor's Degree in Business Management from Saint Peter's University.

She is an active member and a well-regarded leader at her church; she organizes and coordinates multiple fundraisers. She volunteers extensively within her church and network. JD is also a member of the Finance Council and is bilingual allowing her to serve both the English and Spanish communities. She is relied upon as the go-to contact amongst family and friends because of her huge heart and nature to serve others.

She is a Monat Affiliate and is referred to as the Chief of Everything (COE) because of her will and determination to get things done, further demonstrating her versatility and leadership skills in business. She is currently working on scaling non-for-profit businesses to serve; senior citizens, domestic violence victims and resources for the homeless.

In her chapter of the book, JD shares her experiences and insights, offering a unique perspective on resilience and the power of a positive outlook. Her writing style and personal story make her chapter and the book a must-read for anyone seeking guidance and motivation. Her knowledge and accomplishments make her a respected figure in the business community, and her participation in Women's Warrior promises to cement her status as a enterprise-minded leader and inspirational author.

FB: JD JD

IG: @itsjeanettediaz

email: itisjeanettediaz@gmail.com

Thank you, God, for the blessings and lessons. Thank you for your unconditional love. Thank you for knowing the depths of my strengths and pushing me to my limits.

A heartfelt thanks to John, Janiece, Ashley, and Enzo you fill my life with so much love and happiness. Thank you for being my number one advocates, for always being present and for loving me when I couldn't love myself.

Thank you, Jenn, I'm so grateful our paths crossed. We both know the sky is not the limit, after all man has been on the moon. The future is bright! May God continue blessing you immensely.

Chapter 15:
Uninvited

Maureen Richards Spadaro

That was me. I was uninvited to one of my best friend's surprise 60th birthday party. What's worse? I had to accept the truth of how her partner felt about me. How does something like this happen to a woman my age, and by someone I thought of as a friend?

It started innocently enough. My friend Charlotte and I were chatting one day when she asked me if I received the save-the-date to our friend Sarah's surprise party her wife Pat was hosting. Although I hadn't yet received it, I wasn't initially concerned until Charlotte told me she received it 2 weeks earlier via email. I thought that was strange. Did Pat forget to send it? Was it possible I wasn't going to be invited? That thought seemed impossible because I knew Pat well, had worked with her in the past, and as far as I knew we were good. Although it sat uncomfortably within me, I decided to wait until the invites went out to see if perhaps the save-the-date was an oversight.

Sure enough a few weeks later I received a text from Pat about the surprise party. She said she needed my email address, and asked that I not say anything to Sarah about it. As I sent Pat my email address, I reassured her I had heard about the party, spoke with Sarah several times without mentioning it, and her secret was safe with me. I thought it a bit odd that she felt the need to ask me not to tell Sarah. I wasn't known for breaking confidences and ruining surprises. Once again something didn't sit right with me, but I shook it off. I was happy and excited to be attending. Their parties are always beautiful, and I was looking forward to being with friends I hadn't seen for a while and the look on Sarah's face when she walked in. Her 50th had been a beautiful celebration and I was sure this would be another celebration for the books.

Several weeks passed, and life went on as usual. I was in the process of making good on a promise I made to myself that 2023 was the year I was going to find more creative ways to get my book, Press Pause, further out into the world. I came up with the idea to go to the TODAY Show Plaza in NYC with a few books in tow to see if I could get them into the hands of the newscasters and some of the fans in attendance who gathered on the Plaza. The idea felt like an adventure and I was going to ask my friend Jarrod to join me to record it as part of a documentary we were starting to work on. I also thought it would be fun to throw out an invite on my Facebook page to anyone who wanted to join me, transportation and lunch provided. The only information they would be given was the date, which was originally going to be January 27th. After speaking with Jarrod, he wasn't able to do it on the 27th but was free on the February 3rd. I joked I had nowhere to be at 6 a.m. on a Friday so the 3rd would work.

We had the date and a plan, so I actively started to throw out little teasers on my FB page. A few people were interested in coming, and I told them the only thing I could say for sure was we would be going to NYC and leaving very early in the morning. In the end, it was Jarrod and another brave friend who would end up being able to come. Two days after my first "teaser" I was at work when I received a text from Pat. She said she saw I had a big event happening on the 3rd, and wanted to know if I was still going to

Sarah's party. I quickly read the text and panicked. I asked her where she saw it and she said on Facebook. The panic escalated. I jokingly responded "I do?" with an LOL, but was already searching my FB events calendar. I was invited to and agreed to attend a Gala in February, and immediately thought I may have confused the dates of Sarah's party and the Gala. I looked at my FB events and saw the Gala was on the 17th, much to my relief. I reassured Pat that I had absolutely no conflicts with Sarah's party on the 3rd, and that I would be there with bells on.

Another week passed when I was once again at work and heard several messages come through my phone. They were coming in rapidly, but I couldn't look at them right away because I was finishing up a document my boss needed. I was a little concerned with how many were coming through but assumed it was one of three group threads I was a part of. When I had a free moment I opened my phone, glanced down and saw the messages were from Pat.

Her first message was a screenshot of the post I wrote earlier that morning which read: *"GOOD MORNING! My energy is overflowing lately, and I am pushing it all into the Universe and sharing it for anyone who needs it. I'm thinking about my next adventure on February 3rd, and a few thoughts started creeping in..." I'm sure a million other people have thought of this and tried it." "I should figure out something different and unique to do." In the not-so-distant past I would have decided this was a warning and stepped back from it....".* I continued to write about following your dreams, thinking out of the box, and fighting off the fears and doubts.

I wasn't sure why she sent me a screenshot of my own FB post until I read the second text which read: "Is this the big February 3rd event you forgot about?".

February 3rd event? I assured her the only other event I had was on the 17th a week ago. The confusion grew when a screenshot of another one of my posts written a day or two earlier followed. That post read: *"GOOD MORNING! Are you setting your sights on your dreams? My next task takes place on the 3rd. If you read my post about the discomfort I experience asking for something then you know as the day gets closer the doubt and discomfort grows..."*

Pat followed that screenshot with two texts: "Same one? And, you acted as if I was crazy?", followed by "Why is it you have not stopped posting about February 3rd since I invited you and we spoke? What's the MO?"

The MO? I had no MO. I barely had time to read that when a screenshot of yet another one of my FB posts came through followed by Pat's text: "Clearly you have a conflict, so I will change your response."

Change my response? She was uninviting me? I sat at my desk staring at my phone in shock. What conflict? I responded yes - TWICE! Now, she was changing it to no? I was hurt, confused and starting to get angry.

"I have no idea what you are talking about Pat. There are 24 hours in a day. Sarah's party is for six of those hours."

Her response: "You had no idea about an event on the 3rd also, but have posted nonstop. You are a liar; Maureen and you need to get your intentions in the right place. Don't fuck with my wife's party."

The words were said with such disdain, I froze. I had to pause for several minutes and take a breath. I started and stopped several responses but finally answered with "I don't have an event on the 3rd! I am doing something that morning I am excited about. A

227

liar? Because I have something to do the morning of Sarah's party???"

Had she made a note of everyone's FB posts and questioned them about what they were doing the day of the party? I wanted to respond to her that the 3rd wasn't even my first choice but it was the only morning that worked for what I wanted to do, but I stopped myself. I realized I had done nothing wrong and suddenly felt no obligation to explain myself or the plans I made. Two yes responses should have been the end of it. Confusion and anger turned to frustration. From never getting the save-the-date, to being "reminded" not to tell Sarah about her surprise party like I was a child, and then questioning if I was still coming after receiving my response to the e-vite, my patience had run out.

Her next response was simple: "I am not entertaining this bullshit! Cut the shit, Maureen!

It became very clear to me that Pat didn't want me at the party. Calm and prepared I took a deep breath and responded: "And, neither am I, Pat. I said I was coming. What I do before that is my life. This is sick and you are a bully. You clearly invited me because you felt you had to. Consider your obligation fulfilled. What I do at 6 a.m. on the 3rd is my business. I would never fuck with Sarah's party. But, don't think you can fuck with me. You can't."

I steadied myself. I know first-hand what happens when you push back against a bully. You will swear the earth has opened up and is trying to swallow you whole. I was sick of bullies having access to my life. I was sick of feeling I had to placate bullies in order to avoid their wrath. Pat's response simply proved I was right.

"You are a sick, jealous and envious woman. I knew IF I invited you too soon you would try to sabotage her party. And, what a shame, she loves you so much! I invited you because I knew SHE would want me to. Me, not so much. I see the FB games you have played with my wife. You need MAJOR help."

And, there it was. She didn't want me at the party. She never sent me the save-the-date, and it wasn't because she suddenly didn't have my email address. But it was the rest of what she wrote that left me cold. I'm jealous and envious? I need MAJOR help? How can I be jealous when I shared with Sarah any opportunity that came my way to help her build upon the dreams, she still had for herself? How can I be envious when I cried and cheered every single time another one of Sarah's dreams came to fruition. And when did encouraging Sarah to keep going and continue to bring her dreams to life define someone who is sick? I worked for her and willingly invested the time and money to try to become the best producing agent I could be, made countless memories with her and now I am this twisted woman Pat has created in her head? Sarah and I always laughed and told each other we lived parallel lives. Good or bad, if something happened to her, eventually it would happen to me and vice versa. Even before we knew one another the similarities we uncovered about our earlier lives made it seem like we were destined to be friends forever.

I asked myself what brought all of this on. Pat and I were always friends. The last time I saw her was when I brought my mom to visit Sarah at her office and Pam was there. And, the time before that was at their beach house, riding on the back of the wave runner they just bought with Pat, having fun.

I thought about the irony of the situation. It was Sarah who taught me the importance of writing down, repeating and shouting your dreams into the universe. Early on it was her examples that started to make me believe that what I thought about I brought about. Here I was doing just that, finally unafraid, and her wife is calling me a saboteur and a liar.

Red faced with my heart beating from my chest, I took a deep breath and responded: "My MO? Because I am happy and excited about my life? Who are you to control what I do the other 18 hours in my day? Jealous? Sabotage? No worries...you can invent whatever scenario you want. I have loved Sarah forever, and will continue to do so despite your delusions. I wish you well Pat. You cannot begin to fathom how wrong you are. You have the conflict, not me. But I am always happy to know where I stand with people."

The texts stopped. My heart broke. I thought about Sarah and what she would think when she realized I wasn't at her party. I thought about what Pat would say to her or how she would convince Sarah that I somehow was trying to sabotage her night.

For several days following I felt so small and insignificant. What had I ever done that would justify such anger? In the 10 or 11 years I have known Pat we have never had a cross word. In 40+ years of friendship with Sarah, we have had 1 misunderstanding. Where was Pat's rage coming from? Could it have come from that 1 misunderstanding that occurred almost a year ago? I thought Sarah and I had worked through it. Was I wrong? I have no choice but to accept these are questions I cannot answer. Only Pat and Sarah have the answer.

As the days turned to weeks, I made the conscientious decision to continue to dig into my bag of skills, and accept that I have no control over what Pat thinks or says. I stopped my ruminating thoughts about the ugliness of it all, and began focusing that energy on the projects I once hesitated to start. As time has passed, I realize Pat's assumptions and reactions ended up being one of the biggest lessons I still had to learn. I can only control what I think, do and say. Several years ago I would have done anything to explain the misunderstanding, promising with a desperation that I would never lie or hurt either of them. I would have apologized and asked for forgiveness for something I didn't do.

Not this time. Not anymore.

I took the hate and anger Pat attempted to hurt me with, and am using it instead to fuel my dreams. I am immersing myself in the excitement and joy I wish to inspire others to have in their lives.

I am not sure what Sarah thinks or feels. We actually spoke the morning of her party. She wished me good luck on my adventure in New York. She had no idea her party was just hours away. No idea I wouldn't be there. What did she think? Did she think I didn't want to be there? Did she think I was too busy to celebrate her? Did she also believe that I was jealous of her, envious and sick? Had one misunderstanding decided who she believed I was more than 40+ years of friendship? We haven't spoken since that morning. A marriage is a partnership that no one should be able to divide, and I believe and respect that. But I have no tolerance nor is there room in my life for bullies, abusers, or chaos. I have reached a level of emotional freedom I have worked hard to attain my entire life.

People come into our lives for a reason, a season, or a lifetime. Some stay for all. Only the Universe knows if my friendship with Sarah will fulfill all three. And, I understand I have as much to say about that as Sarah. Whatever the outcome I know and believe I will always be exactly where I am supposed to be, surrounded by those who are meant to be in my life. I know who I am. I know the intentions that live in my heart.

No matter what, I will never allow a person to believe they have the final say when it comes to the friend and woman, I know I am.

A motivational speaker, and a surthriver of multiple sexual and domestic violence traumas which began at the age of 6, Maureen released her first book "Press Pause; The Breakdown That Rebuilt My Life & Changed a Family Legacy" in April, 2020. Maureen has shared her message of surthrival and hope as a speaker at Monmouth University, Georgian Court University, both Long Branch and Neptune High Schools in New Jersey, the Attachment and Trauma Network Conference in Washington DC, The Lightworkers Series at the NJ Arts Center, and What's Your Story USA. As a guest on several podcasts and shows including Sonstein Sundays and Women in the Loop on iHeart Radio, Wheelhouse, B*Inspired, and This Is It TV, Maureen's goal is to share what it took for her to go from "emotional and internal deafness" to creating a life she loves. Recently, Maureen was asked to launch her peer-led support group for The Stephanie Parze Foundation, C.O.A.P, founded in the memory of Freehold, NJ resident Stephanie Parze

who was murdered at the hands of her abusive ex-boyfriend, and is a supporter of Bikers Against Child Abuse (BACA).

"The single most important ingredient to moving past trauma or any adversity we face in life is willingness. When you are in the depths of despair, working through grief, starting over, or trying to move beyond any type of trauma words like strength, courage, resilience and hope are impossible to relate to. The pain you are experiencing blocks your ability to see those traits within yourself; traits that exist in all of us. But, willingness? When someone says they are willing, they are saying "I will try". And, each step taken slowly unlocks the strength, courage, resilience and hope we possess. Our willingness to "put me first", do the work required to release the pain we carry, and clear that space within for all the good that awaits to land is the

groundwork we lay in order to build the life we love."

Maureen's dream is to open homes throughout the country, and expand the concept of Marilyn's Place to build a community for survivors of abuse to live, rent free, for a year in order to save their money, or complete school and have a fresh start to create a life they love and deserve, in safe and supportive surroundings.

Thank you to every person who has been kind enough to share with me how my honesty and willingness to talk about my life and my struggles has helped them. It took me decades to find my voice and use it. It's taken me even longer to be proud of who I am and continue to become. Thank you to my family for encouraging me to keep going, even through the financial and sometimes emotional tolls that accompany everyone trying to live in their purpose. And, most importantly, I am grateful to God who quietly spoke to the heart of a frightened little girl and told her it would all be okay one day. It is that belief that has sustained me, and allowed me to try "one more time".

Warm regards,

Maureen Spataro

Author, Press Pause

"I am not braver, stronger or more courageous
than anyone. I am simply willing."

Chapter 16:
Believing In Me from My Younger Self

Lilys Duran

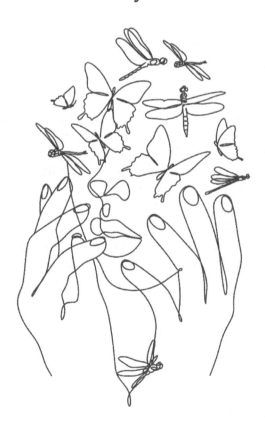

W hy be part of this project?
I sat down to think about the idea of writing a chapter of a book and being part of this amazing project, and as excited as I was, I still doubted myself. Being a part of the first Women Warriors group project is such an opportunity. This idea may mean a lot to many of us, but at the same time we may question ourselves, not knowing where to start or what to write. I thought once, twice and a third time questioning myself for days. After writing down the pros and cons of this project, I realized that opportunities like this don't come to your door often. If they do come to your door most likely, you will say "no". There are a lot of things that were giving me the "Yes" it is possible. Then on the other side, is self-doubt. Am I sure I want to do this?

Yes, I was afraid of the commitment it would bring and the challenges of placing myself outside of my comfort zone. The project and the opportunity is so huge I was trying to find all the excuses to not be part of it because I was scared. I didn't think this was possible for me. However, I have learned that when things get harder it is because there is a greater purpose. It will be so big that you could not even see it. So here I am, being myself, ready to try and believe it is possible. To say, "Wow, I will be part of a book and be considered an author. I'm writing a chapter of a book. Is it possible?" Yes, it's happening!

I'm here, writing now. I don't really know what I'm going to write about, but I can say my heart is so grateful for this opportunity.

I would begin by introducing myself and sharing my why and purpose of my life. I decided to say yes to this amazing opportunity because it will help me become a bigger person. The feeling of having a purpose like most of us do but never talk about it. So one of the things that I want to share here is where I come from, who I am today, and who I plan on becoming. What is my purpose in life? Trust me I don't only have one. So let's start with the way I feel about myself today, because it isn't even close to where I'm going to be and where I want to be. Working hard and being able to accomplish goals and dreams small or big fulfills my soul and takes me there.

If I go back to "Lilys" the little girl, I can say she always had health issues. I was not able to attend school for an entire month because one or two of those weeks I was hospitalized. I remember just being sick, fragile, and skinny. I was not able to create memories with friends, because of my health limitations but I 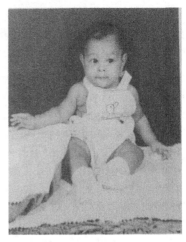 always held on to what I liked. Dancing, playing basketball and volleyball and growing up in a Catholic school. I participated in these sports and activities including marching band known as a "batutera." My parents didn't think that I would grow old so I was not allowed to do much or participate in all activities. The constant asthma attacks, heart murmur, and rheumatic fever to name a few. I needed to drink some of the nastiest home remedies daily in order to control the asthma attacks. Yes, after all these complications, I grew up. This year in April 2023, I will be 50 years old. Those events and struggles made me stronger and I don't regret it. Those experiences made me the person that I am today-a strong woman, a warrior, and most importantly a believer.

Days before my 15th birthday my mother came to the United States, it was hard for all of us because we were always together. At the age of 16, I graduated high school in DR thinking of my dream to become a doctor. I admired my pediatrician, so much for helping me with my illnesses that I wanted to serve and help others, as well. Shortly after my sister (11 years old) and I migrated to the United States with our mom, followed by my dad two years later. I started my first job ever in retail and shortly after registering in the community college to begin to learn English. It was very challenging to start from zero, learning a new culture and not knowing anyone. It was very frustrating for me not being able to communicate in English. My cousins were in the USA longer and my sister learned the language faster than they could speak. When they talked in front of me, I felt uncomfortable.

Making friends was not too difficult for me, I made connections with great people throughout the years. Friends that I still keep in touch with, some became part of my family. I have had a best friend since my first day of college and we are still friends. My oldest daughter Ammie's Godmother is someone that has always been by my side. She is the only person I really go to when I need to speak about anything. It is like a sisterhood of 30 years plus since the moment we met. I think we were there for each other trying to do something new, just as our friendship grew. She was everywhere with me and I was everywhere with her. Her daughter Marlene is a very special person to all of us. I started adapting to this new culture, attempting a modeling career while dating and shortly marrying my husband. The year after my first child Ammie was born, I took a break in college but went back two years later. My daughter Lindsey was born in 1998 while finishing college. In 2001, I started working at the local hospital where I did for many years. During that period of time, I had to care for my father after he suffered a massive heart attack. After weeks in ICU, undergoing a very risky open-heart surgery and a long, slow recovery.

My sister and I had always taken care of our parents, checking on them daily and giving everything, they needed. They were both by our side helping us accomplish our goals and with our daily lives. My dad had a couple of emergencies but he was considered stable and he was a very active man. After my son Gabriel was born, I received an opportunity to continue my education by becoming a Community Doula. I met and worked with amazing women with different stories. My mentors were Registered Nurses that love and dedicated years of their lives to their careers. Ms. Marie and Mrs. Christine taught and guided me to lead others as well as to be more confident. I started working a part-time job as a community doula and months later I was offered a full-time position, resigning to my job at the hospital.

I was working from home, visiting pregnant women at their homes, helping them understand and prepare for labor. This is a very rewarding job for me where I realized how much I love to help others. I began to see more clearly my purpose in life.

About seven years ago, my mom was diagnosed with breast cancer. Thank god it was detected at a very early stage. She underwent surgery on the area and had radiation therapy only. She was positive at all times and accepted all decisions with the best attitude but not knowing what was coming our way. My paternal grandfather living in the Dominican Republic was worried about my mom since the moment he found out she had surgery to remove cancer. Little did we know that it was going to be affecting his health. One afternoon while at work my sister and I received multiple phone calls from the Dominican Republic which we missed or couldn't hear anything. Our grandfather, with the help of our little cousin, was trying to get in touch with us to ask about my mom. He thought we were not telling him the truth about her health. A couple of hours later, we received the call that he passed away at the hospital. While my heart was broken, I had to give the news to my mother. It was devastating for me. We were not able to travel leaving our mother behind recovering from surgery.

The resilience I have in my life are the results of failures, frustrations and experiences. Writing about those struggles and sad moments is hard. I know I am not alone in the reason why I feel the need to share. Growth!! A lot of growth, a lot of hard moments, a long journey. This is what life is all about.

Today, I look back to my past to cry or laugh and I can say, I consider myself happy, even though happiness are moments that we gather together. I don't think everybody is happy all the time because life is full of ups and downs. Happiness is what you make it and what you believe it is. It's having a reason to smile, laugh, run, cry. We all have days, we don't want to get out of bed, but we do things that make us feel better. Not too long ago, I realized that my feelings matter. If I want to be by myself or I would like to listen to music, I want to dance in the rain then I am able to. It's about how it makes me feel and I am important. I have a lot of people that are so important in my life. But I have to start with myself. I cannot give any quality of time or love to others if I'm not good on my own. Believe it or not, I always felt low self-esteem even though a lot of people thought of me as the opposite. I was always rushing, letting everyone around me pull me and push me as they pleased without a real reason. Now, I feel different and with a purpose. It took me a long time to realize what it was. I believe now I can achieve whatever I want and put myself out there.

I always worked hard but I used to leave everything halfway. This time around, I'm working on myself every single day. I am focused on the future, my purpose and on what I want to accomplish. I take it one day at a time, life is not easy and goals may be hard to accomplish. I have learned that the people around you have to be a plus in your life and not a minus, they cannot make you who you are. When you are comfortable with yourself then you know you can influence others. For many years, people in my life have wanted to influence or change me if you can call it that way. They wanted me to be what they wanted me to be. Everything changed the day I decided to put myself first then the rest.

My real journey started the day I accepted God as my Lord and Savior. I opened my heart, soul and mind to Him. The day I let God guide my life, opened my arms to accept the great things I deserve and the path I needed to follow. I thank God for the way I think and feel now. Learning to care for myself more was a huge step. It did happen slowly and today I am proud.

Everything I have in my life gives me the strength to continue, it gives me peace and makes me grow. I can laugh with joy. I have a dream. I have goals. I am being myself with a humble and grateful heart, always willing to help, to give my hand to whoever needs it. Sometimes people are in desperate need and they don't feel comfortable asking for help, I was one myself. I have learned throughout the years that I have to be ready to give, but also to receive. I was always doing everything myself and not letting anyone know that I needed help, which drove me to be overwhelmed, and stressed with anxiety. I wanted to do it all and didn't want to disappoint the rest of the world. I wanted it right, I wanted perfect. I created expectations in my mind and assumed others would give me their hand if I needed it. One of the things that was very hard for me to accept is that people thought that I could get and go through everything without tears in my eyes. People thought that I didn't have feelings or that I could handle anything. On my hardest times, I cried alone. I probably showed myself to others as a strong and powerful person at all times. I didn't show my feelings in public and tend to cry in the shower or in my bedroom. I called them my "war room" where I pray and talk to God. Going through a lot of challenges and not having someone's hand or shoulder was difficult. But I learned to cope and take care of myself. Then, that became a problem because the moment I started to say no to others, I became a selfish person. I never thought it was going to be possible, a people's person like me was always available 24/7. I made changes that made me be a better me. Yes, I'm doing things for me and it feels so good. I created boundaries and I am no longer surrounded by everybody's energy. I'm more relaxed and a better listener. I make changes and things are different. I'm capable of doing anything that I want and that I deserve. As a parent, I always wanted to do things differently and didn't want to raise my kids how I was raised. I wanted to support them in their dreams, careers and goals. I wanted to be their friend without being a parent. Able to have good communication so that we could sit down to have difficult conversations. As a parent you don't want to hear others say bad things about your children. I showed them the good way to live their lives. I have never let others intervene into our relationships, it's about them and I. I may hear someone's advice but will no longer let anyone decide for me.

In my path, I have learned that reading is a way of growing, of living through others experiences. I have been trying to be better at reading, be more focused to better myself and to keep a routine. I think we start doing things differently when we are hungry for more, with a dream of becoming an intrapreneur and have our own business. That's the mindset, the vision and goal to not live paycheck to paycheck. It took me a long time to find something that I enjoy to work with. I tried a couple of direct sales companies

245

unsuccessfully and other different business ideas. I was so hungry to find the right business that I tried not only once, but twice and failed. I didn't accomplish or gain much out of that. I had motivation but not enough to last. Nothing that could help me to be consistent and to be resilient. Nothing that pushed me to think bigger or to have a clear vision of what I wanted to do. I learned how to try harder even though I was doing it with the right people, it was not with the right company. While looking for more business ideas, the world started changing. We were going through a pandemic that made us slow down. I found what was going to fulfill me, my hunger for more and keep me busy during this time. It helped me build a confidence, mindset, and made me feel aligned. I joined a Network Marketing Company to help women feel better with themselves. I am affiliated with Monat, a global leader in naturally based, anti-aging products. I was so excited for this business opportunity and the amazing products that I wanted to bring my circle of friends and family to become part of this and achieve success together. I shared my vision, time, dreams and goals with many as well as celebrated all of our successes. I started networking, meeting people, building a presence in social media as well as going to events and trips. I'm here pushing harder to become better than I was yesterday. These couple of years I have experienced wins and failures that have taught me that you should try again tomorrow. Not giving up on the right things is what matters. Everybody has to fight daily and only needs to know how to react to that fight. Breathe, meditate, take a break and then go back to it. My stress level years ago was up to the roof, the reason why everything went wrong. At least, I saw it going wrong but the moment I shifted, things started opening up.

I started to do things differently, still hungry, always with a dream of becoming an intrapreneur to have my own successful business, a mindset, a vision but with a more focused purpose. It's about this huge opportunity of sharing your feelings, sharing your experiences and your story. It is never too late to keep grinding, keep going, pushing through and working towards your dreams. Yeah, maybe my dream is to become a better me every day. I'm not giving up. Success is celebrating the small wins and creating small goals. It's having a plan but most important working towards it. Knowing how to execute, learning from those days you fail, focusing your energy mentally and physically is going to keep you up. I get up everyday with the best mindset of accomplishing a lot every single day even if it doesn't go well. I keep in mind that things happen for me, not to me. I talk to myself a lot because I'm my biggest cheerleader. It is not my ego; it's patting myself on the back because I'm a big deal. At the end of the day being wise, being better, doing better, feeling better and having lots of fun is necessary. Thank God, I am surrounded by the right people; people that are supportive, without any doubt, people that even though they are not there, they want you to get there, people that may be grateful because I'm in their lives, but I'm more grateful to have them. We all need to go through the process hard or not because nothing worth it is easy. Good intentions and a grateful heart is key. We cannot change people but we can't let people change us either. If someone doesn't treat me well, I pray for them. I believe in people, friendship, family regardless if I was hurt by any of them. I realized everybody goes through stages and relationships have seasons. I count my blessings every single day because I have way more things than what I need. One of the things that took me longer to accept is that I deserve everything and more. It took me to read a lot of books, listen to many podcasts about how we need to love ourselves, that we deserve every single good thing that happened to us. And probably the bad in a sense just to make us learn from it.

This is the reason why today I said if it didn't happen it is because of a reason. Probably my purpose in life was different. So never regret what you didn't do because there is always time to do something bigger. That's how I feel that I'm doing now, when I am looking back it's like a lot of things I didn't do and I missed but it's never too late to do great. Never in a million years thought that I'll be where I am today.

I do have a lot of great friends which at times were great. Sometimes we grew apart because we no longer have the same vision and the same purpose in life. God has blessed me with great people. Regardless if they're here today with me or not, the moment we were and the time was perfect. But today, what I want and how I feel is different, not that everything has to be related to money to feel great but accomplishing something big towards your dream. Your hard work will get you where you want to go. I'm a mother of three. Three different individuals with different personalities, they're brothers and sisters. Everybody has their moments and the time they need me, I'm there. I was always running around with my kids. We forgot a little bit about our things to enjoy our family times with them. We dedicated our lives to fulfill our kids' lives and their activities.

Today, I'm a little more careful about bringing people around me, not because I gave up friendships, but because I'm protecting my energy, mental health, environment, keeping a little bit more space, and with the same love. I do show a thicker skin not as thick as what people see.

After all the personal development and all the neat things, I am taking time to take a nap, have a glass of wine, watch a movie by myself, go to bed early or not go to bed on time, and go out with your friends. You know, I feel good. So I don't know which world I was living in before now, but I can say it feels good here. Now I know that I have grown.

The year 2022, taught me great things but very tough ones as well. My health was going backwards, having to take care and focus myself and on getting better. The moment I thought things were going in the right direction, I got sick again, problems with my breathing, etc. Not knowing how the year was going to end. At the end of October, shortly after me, my mother got sick, followed by my dad. Things shifted very fast and his health was deteriorating. My world was shaking again, ICU memories coming back, anxiety, stress on top of my breathing problems. I didn't recognize myself at moments of how fragile and worried I had become. Making hard decisions, listening constantly to medical diagnosis, longer days, sleepless, restless and forgetting about me. Days passed listening to the worse, imagining an end and praying even harder to stay strong. Those days were not getting better but dough was not an option and praying was the answer. Letting God do and stop worrying, believing in his promise was the only way of keeping me breathing. Not knowing my priorities, protecting my mom and family with hope. Keeping myself and my business alive, showing up to others even when I couldn't show up to myself. Repeating a loud "God is Good all the time" to convince myself and assured my sister everything will be okay.

Lilys Duran was born in the Dominican Republic in April 11, 1973. She migrated with her parents and her little sister to the United States of America at the age of 16. She worked in retail while attending a Community College to learn the English language and earn her degree. She is a woman of faith, wife, and mother of two girls and a boy (Ammie, Lindsey and Gabriel).

She has a special love for Science, Art & Community.

First, I thank God for always placing me around amazing people and great places. Without God, nothing would have been possible for me. I want to thank my wonderful husband and our three amazing children for their patience and encouragement. My parents, my sister, my niece and nephew. My cousin Viancey Peraza, for her unconditional support. My best friend Carmen Cruz, for always checking on me. My closest friends for their support on good and not so good days and believing I can do it. To those that are no longer part of my circle of friends, thank you for the experiences and lessons learned because those have taught me to love myself even more.

Chapter 17: Don't Let Fear Catch Your *Tongue*

Lisa Marie Falbo

It's been three years since my husband, Joe, and I journeyed the long, windy road to our favorite getaway spot, The Lodge at Woodloch. This Pennsylvania treasure is where we love to relax, recharge, and reconnect. The fact that we could carve out this time was a minor miracle, between the hustle and bustle of our respective businesses and caring for our gorgeous, rambunctious toddler, Liana. But a rebalancing of the scales was in order; in a few short months, we will add to the chaos with our second baby.

As we approached the familiar grand entrance, I could already feel the stresses of life melting away. But as we unloaded our overnight bags and faced the Lodge's wooden walkway, I felt a bittersweetness. Was it the pregnancy hormones? Was it the guilt of leaving Liana overnight for the first time? Was it the worry of a work task being missed while I was gone?

No. It was none of those things. It was me finally honoring all that had changed since the last time I stood here.

January 1, 2020, was the last time I breathed in this crisp mountain air. At the time, everything seemed perfect—Joe and I were married a year prior, and we were living my dream life in Jersey City, overlooking the iconic Manhattan skyline. Together we had active, full lives yet gave each other the freedom to chase our dreams, a necessity of two independent Sagittarians like us.

But even amidst the idyllic setting, I remember sensing a foreboding presence lurking around the corner. At the start of a new year, I like to visualize what I want the next 365 days to look like. But here, my vision was something other than 20/20.

Upon returning home, I got an answer to the unsettled vibes I was feeling— the pregnancy I learned about at the end of 2019 was not viable. I had a "missed miscarriage," where the baby died, but my body did not realize it. We got the shocking news during an ultrasound appointment, and I spent our first wedding anniversary later that week passing it naturally.

While still grappling with this monumental loss, the COVID-19 pandemic hit, forcing everyone to shut down for two weeks. Initially, I was pleased (and admittedly, a little relieved) with the break, oblivious to the subconscious changes that would eventually turn my world upside down.

I eagerly spent those 14 days tackling long-ignored items on my to-do list while enjoying some "me" time. I found renewed vigor in my purpose, and it felt like those beginning, exciting days of my entrepreneurial journey when I would work 25 hours a day from my parent's guest bedroom.

As the lockdown extended, I only became more inspired. I created a podcast called *Live from My Living Room*, where I Zoomed with people from around the world about this weird time in history and how they were navigating our "new normal." I pivoted in my business, Long Shot Productions, by taking all my video work to the online streaming world and locally televising these projects. I didn't realize it then, but making the most out of the pandemic built up the confidence and resiliency I would later need.

On May 27, 2020, I had to deal with another monumental change. I moved from my beloved Jersey City and boomeranged back to my hometown of East Hanover. We had purchased a house a year prior and underwent a rigorous renovation project. The promise of our beautiful "forever home" house was tempered by the emotional toll of leaving behind cherished memories; it was the end of a lifelong dream I was not ready to give up.

As we settled into our new home, I started to feel the pressure of society ever-so-slowly reopening. I put tremendous pressure on myself to get "back to normal, back to work" while navigating ever-changing protocols and delicate psyches. I couldn't help but feel, once again, an ominous shift in the air. It was as if the world around me was slowly but surely crumbling, leaving me in perpetual unease. My life had become a flurry of emotional turbulence, with one difficult week following another.

Despite the success of my business lockdown projects, professional relationships were deteriorating. I was pouring my heart and soul into every production, and I realized with growing dismay that the effort was not reciprocated. I felt a growing isolation and disappointment. I realized that I had always been the one to provide unwavering support and encouragement for others' endeavors with no respect given to mine. It was a hard truth to swallow, but I knew what to do. I summoned the courage to have some difficult conversations and made overdue decisions that I always knew in my heart that I had to make but always avoided to keep the peace.

Despite these betrayals and the debilitating anxiety, I fought on. Don't get me wrong; making these decisions with no plan was scary. However, a colleague summarized my situation perfectly, and I will never forget it: "They may be left with the Ferrari, but you are taking the engine." That encouragement and the goodwill I built up during those lockdown days carried me during those precarious last months of 2020.

When the pruning of my proverbial tree was complete, the universe started responding by leveling up all areas of my life.

On July 22, 2020, I once again found myself on an examination table waiting to get a pregnancy confirmed via ultrasound. Even though I figured I could get good news since I was so physically ill, the memory of the missed miscarriage was still fresh. I braced for impact as the technician worked her wand. Imagine my shock when she said, "Congratulations!" My eyes flung open, and I turned my head toward the screen and saw a tiny gingerbread-looking figure lazily floating about. Eight months later, on March 4, 2021, we welcomed Liana Lucille Falbo into the world.

Needing to build my business team basically from scratch, I made sure to surround myself with good-intentioned gems of people that have helped grow Long Shot into heights only imagined (our three New York Emmy nominations since 2021 only tell part of the tale). The good vibes of aligning myself with true partnerships reached all the way to Chicago, where a broadcast group took notice of a new streaming show I was co-producing and hosting called the *New Jersey Morning Show*. They wanted us to create all their Garden State content on a local television station they had purchased. Contracts were signed in a matter of days, and another LLC was created. By January 2022, my Long Shot space was transformed into the bustling Media First Group newsroom, where creativity and positivity flowed.

The most exciting part of the deal was that I was gifted with my weekend television show, *Your New Jersey*, where I speak with community do-gooders throughout the Garden State. To have this opportunity in the New York market is an absolute dream fulfilled. The most significant feedback I get from viewers is that I radiate joy on screen, and I know they are telling the truth because I genuinely am on the show and in everything I do now.

The biggest takeaway I've carried since those turbulent times of 2020 is when you immediately see something that violates your integrity, say something. Take people for what they are, and do not romanticize them. Being overly nice to difficult personalities gets you nowhere, only grief. And if you are holding on to something that isn't serving you, don't be afraid to let go. You will be paid back for shedding the dead weight in dividends.

In business and life, don't let fear catch your tongue.

Emmy-Nominated Host and Executive Producer; Author Lisa Marie Falbo is an Emmy-nominated television host, entrepreneur, and author. A dynamic force in the media world, she has overseen numerous corporate and television productions while serving as a host for various television and digital programs.

Since 2009, Lisa Marie has served as founder and CEO of **Long Shot Productions**, a full-service corporate video production company based in Fairfield, New Jersey. Additionally, she is a partner of Media First Group, specializing in television production for broadcast, cable, and streaming platforms. Through these ventures, her career has spawned numerous commercial, corporate, and entertainment projects that have taken her throughout the United States and Europe.

Lisa Marie's upbeat attitude and curious nature have served her well in front of the camera. Currently, she hosts "**Your New Jersey**" on MeTV-WJLP, which features community leaders throughout the Garden State. A proud Italian-American, she also serves as co-host of "**The Italian America Show**" on News 12+.

Lisa Marie has been nominated for numerous New York Emmy Awards. In 2021, she was lauded for her host and executive producer roles in Alzheimer's New Jersey's "We Take Care of Our Own" televised benefit. In 2022, two of her projects, "Bounce Out the Stigma" with Eisai, Inc. and "Women's

Entrepreneurship Week at Montclair State University," were recognized.

In 2016, Lisa Marie published her first novel titled **"Ten Years Later."** In 2017, the book won Best Fiction at the Independent Authors Book Expo.

Lisa Marie has appeared on a wide variety of local television, network cable, radio shows, and print publications, including TLC's "Cake Boss," SNY's "Oh Yeah," and WFAN Sports Radio Boomer and Carton Show.

Lisa Marie spent 15 years working as a radio producer for WFAN Sports Radio 660AM and the New York Giants Radio Network.

A proud alumna of Montclair State University, she graduated with a broadcasting and speech communication degree in 2006.

In 2021, she and her husband, Joseph, welcomed their daughter, Liana Lucille.

Facebook/Twitter/Instagram/LinkedIn   - @LisaMarieFalbo

Chapter 18:
Life Well $pent

Lynette Barbieri

The first word that comes to mind when I think about entrepreneurship is "warrior." Whatever obstacles you had to overcome, every female entrepreneur got to where she is now by being a warrior.

Women are the glue that holds everything together. We are mothers, sisters, daughters, friends, caregivers, and breadwinners. Some of us have experienced trauma, some have physical or mental illnesses, while others care for sick loved ones. All of our hardships are valid, and we face them while juggling the responsibilities of managing ourselves, our families, and our businesses, regardless of what's going on in our lives.

Every warrior's path is unique, and we all have story to tell. When we exchange these stories and the lessons they offer, we support one another's growth. That's my motivation for sharing my story with you today.

I was born in Brooklyn, New York, and raised in Staten Island, with a brief two-year stretch in Marlboro, New Jersey. I attended a Catholic high school where we were required to wear a uniform every day except Fridays. So, naturally, what I was going to wear on "Friday" was what I had planned my entire week around.

As you might expect, I was never much of a schoolgirl. To me, it was just a social gathering. In fact, I wanted to be a Psychologist until I realized how much schooling was required.

When I graduated from high school at the age of 17, my father informed me that if I continued my education and found a job, he would pay for a college of my choice. I couldn't pass up that opportunity, so when I noticed a sign for Bryman Medical School while passing through East Brunswick, New Jersey, I stopped, got a brochure, and took it home.

It sounded simple enough: I show up and pass, become a medical assistant, and they place me in a job near me where I can make money in a year. So that's exactly what I did. While working my full-time job six days a week, I learned how to collect blood, X-rays, and EKGs.

I worked so hard that the doctor who trained me volunteered to send me to school and pay for my education to become a Nurse Practitioner. The only issue (which turned out to be a significant one) was that I couldn't handle being around sick people.

Working in healthcare requires a special type of person with skills that cannot be taught, and while it made me appreciate people who work in the industry even more, I had to decline the offer.

My parents had divorced at this point in my life, and with so much going on at home, they weren't as focused on what I was doing, which had the unintended benefit of allowing me to try out different occupations. For a time, I worked in a clothing store, a shoe store, and as an assistant in New York City's garment district. I tried numerous jobs, but none satisfied my parents or made me happy.

Then, my beloved grandfather said something that would stick with me forever. "Lynette, you are so beautiful. You could marry any doctor or lawyer you want. What are you doing with your life?" he asked. He never suggested I could be a doctor, a lawyer, or anything else I wanted to be, but he did often compliment me on my intelligence and beauty. When and where he grew up, it was all about going to school, getting married, and raising children. That was all my grandfather knew. Deviating from the standard made no sense to him because anything different was impractical.

My father, on the other hand, was a white-collar worker on Park Avenue in New York City when I was a kid, but he always fantasized about starting his own business. He married when he was 23, had my sister and me, went to college at night to better himself, and provided for us. He had always worked on the side in the hopes of transitioning, but he was making good money, and his main priority was to put food on the table. Years later, after my parents split, Dad left his company and became very successful in real estate, achieving his dream of no longer having a boss. It's safe to say I inherited the "dare to dream" gene from him.

When I was 21, I met my husband, who was working at a well-known Brooklyn pizzeria while saving up to start his own. A few months after we started dating, a friend approached him with an offer, and they opened a pizzeria on St. Marks Place in the Village with a few friends. We were married within a year.

I still wasn't sure who I was or what kind of career I wanted to pursue, so when he suggested that it would be great if I ran the business with him, I agreed. Together, we commuted from Staten Island's southernmost point to the East Village six (long) days a week to run the shop, and we frequently went to McSorley's Ale House after work to unwind.

After a year of doing that, we sold the business and, along with a friend and a partner from the pizzeria, purchased a deli in Brooklyn. We operated it for around seven years, during which I had two daughters and relocated from a Staten Island condo to a home in Old Bridge, New Jersey. I quickly learned how challenging it was to look after two toddlers while accompanying my husband to run our Brooklyn-based business, but I was certain that staying at home and attending playgroups like the other mothers I knew was not for me. I couldn't go back to my job as a medical assistant, but I also couldn't sustain the schedule we were on. I was worn out, and my husband felt the same way.

We were stuck. We liked running a business together and wanted to keep doing so, but there was no way we could keep burning the candle at both ends. We longed for a solution, and on what appeared to be a routine day, one came in the form of a phone call. The person on the other end of the line claimed to work with a financial firm that could help us learn more about money. They also indicated there was an opportunity to work with them part-time, and if we were interested, they would provide the necessary training and credentials. My husband asked them how much we could make, and when they replied that we could make as much we wanted, he invited them over.

I had no intention of joining because, back then, I didn't care about money unless I was spending it. But my husband persuaded me to sit down, and I will always be grateful that he did because I now realize that if my husband had ever left for work and didn't come back, I would have had to sell our home and move back in with a parent.

After that meeting, we sat down to discuss our financial needs, wants, ambitions, and priorities. The first thing we did was put our life insurance into effect so that, in the event of either of us passing away, the other would be able to live in the home and comfortably care for our children. It felt incredible to learn and get on track with our finances, and we knew if we got licensed, we could help our loved ones do the same.

I reluctantly agreed to attend licensing school and training with my husband, but I vowed never to give a speech in front of a group of people or attend in-person appointments. I didn't think I knew enough to impart knowledge to others. I still saw myself as the person who could marry a wealthy business owner, not as the wealthy business owner myself. I was unknowingly projecting sexist attitudes onto myself, which I now recognize was a result of internalized sexism, a problem that so many men and women face but are often unaware of.

Luckily, after attending a few training sessions and passing all of my exams, I realized that I knew so much more than the average person did about money. The more I learned, the more confident I felt in my ability to instruct others. And now? You couldn't shut me up about it if you tried. The girl who swore never to speak in front of a crowd (which, by the way, I still don't love) ended up conducting educational seminars for women, leading group trainings, and giving speeches at big events.

I hope you'll learn what I did from this experience, which is that we are products of what we are told as children until we dare to tell ourselves something different. You must let go of what your grandparents expected of you because they were still products of what they were told. If you want to change your life, you have to change your beliefs. It wasn't until I saw myself as a successful business owner that I could become her.

It won't happen overnight. First, you have to acknowledge that your self-defeating thoughts are not your own. Then, you have to do the work. For me, that meant changing the way I spoke about myself, the way I carried myself, who I hung out with, and what types of content I consumed. One of the first books I read during this time was Napoleon Hill's "Think and Grow Rich." It reinforced what I was discovering for myself, namely, that we can become anything we desire if we're willing to do what it takes to get there. This knowledge gave me the power I needed to take control of my story. Which began chaotic, just like any success story.

I got pregnant with my son shortly after starting licensing school, so this new chapter began with three toddlers. In less than a year, we sold our deli to focus on running the financial company full-time, sold our house, and moved back to Staten Island to live with my mother while we had a new home constructed in New Jersey. I call this chapter, 'Balls to the Wall.'

The toughest jobs require the strongest support systems, and mine proved to be invincible. My sister always stepped in when I needed her. She also had young children, so we switched off whenever we could to help one another. My mother was my backbone. She kept me strong, believed in me, and did everything she possibly could to help out. She always found time to look after her grandchildren while working full-time as a legal secretary for the state of New York. After a twelve-hour day of coordinating and hosting a speaking event, I can clearly recall how secure it made me feel to see my mom waiting for my husband and me in the hotel restaurant or pool, giggling with the kids. She was truly our rock.

Within four years of starting the business, I was able to make a six-figure income, train a team of people and open a beautiful office 3 miles from my home. All three of our children were finally attending school full-time, and the years of chaos were starting to pay off. But the universe must have known that I performed best under pressure because it surprised us with a fourth child. Our moment of peace turned out to be the eye of the hurricane, and we wouldn't have had it any other way. Our wacky little family was complete with the arrival of our youngest daughter, and we knew it was time to adapt once more.

Looking back, I have no idea how I managed to run a company, manage a staff, and raise four kids under the age of nine. But I did it. I persevered with the encouragement of my loved ones and my faith in myself. I've come across a lot of ladies over the years who have used their kids as a justification for not being able to follow their dreams. Please pay attention to me if you are reading this and you catch yourself using the same defense. I promise you'll discover a solution if you shift your viewpoint and consider your children as the "why" you must make it happen for yourself rather than the "why" you can't.

Just as we were getting comfortable with our schedules as a family of six, a devastating blow happened to our family. My husband and I began operating a second office in Staten Island, where I would go once a week and grab lunch with my mother and grandmother. I cherished these little lunch dates but started to notice strange changes in my mother's behavior. After talking with my sister, we decided to take her to the doctor. She saw several specialists that year before receiving an Alzheimer's diagnosis and ultimately had to retire at the young age of 62.

I had to figure out how to help my mom, my kids, and and my business at the same time. My husband was quick to handle everything at work and care for our children when she needed me most, but I still had a responsibility to be a mom and show up as a boss.

I took her to a variety of studies and alternative medical practitioners, but the disease got progressively worse. Although I believe we prolonged it, we could never stop it, and it was becoming harder to manage. To balance some of the responsibilities and get my mother the consistent attention she required and deserved, we wound up hiring caretakers 5 years ago, and we all took care of her until she passed this January. Even though it was difficult to watch her go through that, I miss her every single day and I will never regret the extra time we were allowed to spend together. Time that, if I had been working for someone else, I probably wouldn't have been able to devote.

My life's trajectory was about to change again in 2012, but this time for the better. My children were getting a little older, and I was in a lull with my business. I was itching for a side hustle, so I made the decision to start a networking group. I posted it on Meetup.com under the name "The Freehold Think Tank for Moms," along with a couple dates when everyone could gather at my office.

One of the RSVPs I had received came from a journalist who thought it was a great idea and wanted to cover it for the local paper. I tried to discourage her and invite her to my Women & Money Workshop instead, which I knew would be a packed event, but that didn't interest her at all. She arrived at the networking event with her camera, sat in the back, took pictures, and left without saying a word.

Unbeknownst to me, I was on the cover of the following newspaper, which contained an article about my group. Vanessa Coppes called me after seeing the article, and I'll never forget our first conversation. She started by saying, "hi, you're going to think I'm crazy," to which I responded, "that's okay. I'm crazy, too."

She went on to explain how her husband had left the newspaper in the bathroom, and when she noticed that the front page was advertising a group for mothers starting businesses, she knew she had to meet me. She owned a jewelry business while managing social media for BELLA Magazine and raising her two toddlers. Her family had just moved to the area and didn't have family or friends in New Jersey.

She made numerous perceptive remarks and posed several thought-provoking questions at the first event she attended. Not long after, we met for breakfast and had a lengthy conversation. I was blown away by the amount of enthusiasm and ideas she brought. I remember thinking, "wow, where did this chick come from?!" She even had a suggestion about my hair, which I wasn't sure how to take at the time, but I was intrigued! She was clever, ambitious, and confident, so it was a no-brainer to partner with her.

Now, timing is everything because, a few years prior, I wouldn't have entertained the idea. If I ever entered into partnerships, they were always within my company, and I preferred being in charge. Also, our ages were more than ten years apart, our professions were unrelated, and her children were babies while mine were in middle and high school. We seemed to discover more contrasts the more we spoke, but we shared the important similarities: we were both driven mothers with Type A personalities, and our overarching objective was to support female entrepreneurs.

When I needed her in my life, she appeared. My business was becoming routine, my mother was getting worse, my kids were involved in their sports and hobbies, and I yearned for a project to pour my passion into.

Over the past 11 years, I have gained so much knowledge from this woman and met so many beautiful people. She's the epitome of never giving up, a wonderful mother, loyal, and always there for me. She gave me a new purpose when I needed it. We both believe everything happens for a reason, and everything transpired just as it was meant to.

When she bought the magazine three years ago, she offered the opportunity to work with her in sales. It made sense to give it a shot because I had been attending events with her for eight years, we were co-running ETTWomen and knew we worked well together. Who would have thought I would fall in love with it, go beyond just sales, and become the Business Development Director in three short years? Apparently, she did. She wanted me to join the BELLA Team because she believed in me and saw what I couldn't, and I'll always be grateful for the opportunity.

But opportunities alone won't help us achieve our goals. We must be receptive to the opportunities around us. No matter how far we've come, we must always be willing to learn from others. Almost 25 years ago, when the financial business made the first call, I was eager to try something new and in need of a change. I was willing to listen when Vanessa called and said, "You're going to think I'm crazy." I was willing to challenge myself when I was given the opportunity to work with BELLA and learn something that was absolutely out of my comfort zone at 50 plus.

Everybody experiences difficulties and setbacks; what counts is how you respond to them. If you open the door when opportunity knocks and you continue to answer that door despite the hardships you are facing, you will always find a way. Surrounding yourself with like-minded women that are going to build you up and have your back is also crucial. I have been able to realize my wildest aspirations while raising a beautiful family thanks to the help of my circle. My oldest, Jenna, runs her own business as a mom of two beautiful girls. My second daughter, Danielle, is an Occupational Therapist for the state of NY. My son, Michael, is a successful serial entrepreneur, and my baby is going to college to be a special needs teacher. My husband and I still run our financial business together, and although he didn't always understand why it's important for me to do the other things that I do, he supports me no matter what.

Regardless of how you got to where you are, you did it by being a warrior. The most effective resource a warrior entrepreneur can have is financial literacy, so these five financial fundamentals are what I want to leave you with. You put a lot of effort into getting here, and the last thing you want is to leave your family or yourself vulnerable to financial insecurity in the future.

If you are like most people, you probably know little about finance. The reality is that financial security is attainable for everyone, regardless of income level. You just have to be willing to learn and apply these 5 principles. I'm hopeful they will help you as they've helped my family.

1. The High Cost of Waiting:

By the time you're 67, do you want to have $1 million saved? Start immediately, please! The sooner you begin saving, the less you'll need to put away each month to reach your retirement objectives. It will be more difficult to come up with money for savings the longer you put it off. Save yourself the expensive cost of waiting!

2. Pay Yourself First:

Think you don't make enough money to grow your savings account? Think again! Place your name at the top of the list and treat it like a bill on your budget sheet. Here's what can happen when you save just $100 a month for 40 years:

- At three percent interest, you would have about $93,000.
- At five percent interest, you'd have about $153,240.
- If you received a nine percent interest, you'd have about $472,000.

That's the power of paying yourself first! And remember, it's not what you earn- it's what you keep!

3. The Theory of Decreasing Responsibility -

According to the Theory of Decreasing Responsibility, your need for life insurance peaks along with your family responsibilities. When you're young, you may have children to support, a new mortgage payment, and many other obligations. Yet, you haven't had the time to accumulate much money. This is the time when the death of a breadwinner or caretaker could be devastating and when you need coverage the most. When you're older, you usually have fewer dependents and fewer financial responsibilities. Plus, you've had years to accumulate wealth through savings and investments. At this point, your need for insurance has reduced dramatically, and you have your own funds to see you through your retirement years. It's important to determine the best approach to building wealth while making sure you and your family are protected with the proper amount of life insurance, while you are saving up for future retirement needs.

4. The Rule of 72 -

Do you know the Rule of 72? This rule will genuinely change your life.

It's an easy way to calculate just how long it's going to take for your money to double. Just take the number 72 and divide it by the interest rate you hope to earn. That number gives you the approximate number of years it will take for your investment to double. For example: If your money was earning 3%, you would divide 3 into 72. That equals 24. So, in 24 years your money would double.

If you put away 10,000 dollars at 24 years old and earned 3% interest on that money, you would have 20,000 thousand dollars in 24 years at 48 years old. But, if you put away 10,000 dollars at 24 years old and earned 6% on your money, 6 divided by 72 equals 12. In 12 years when you are 36 years old your money would have doubled to 20,000 dollars, and in 12 more years when you are 48 years old you would have 40,000 dollars.

The Power of Compound Interest shows how you can really put your money to work and watch it grow. When you earn interest on savings, that interest then earns interest on itself and this amount is compounded monthly. The higher the interest, the more your money grows!

5. Debt Stacking -

By taking into account the interest rate and amount of debt, debt stacking identifies a way for you to pay off your debts. You begin by making consistent payments on all of your debts. The debt that debt stacking suggests that you pay off first is called your target account. When you pay off the target account, you roll the amount you were paying toward your next target account. As each debt is paid off, you continue this process. Debt stacking allows you to make the same total monthly payment each month toward all of your debt and works best when you do not accrue any new debts.

You continue this process until you have paid off all of your debts. When you finish paying off your debts, you can apply the amount you were paying towards your debt toward creating wealth and financial independence!

One of the most important building blocks in establishing a firm financial foundation is determining the difference between "wants" and "needs." Sounds simple, doesn't it? A "want" is something you don't require for basic survival, and a "need" is something you must have to live. It can be hard to tell where a "want" begins, and a "need" ends - especially where immediate family is concerned. But you don't have to be perfect. Financial health is all about the choices you make over the long term.

Warriors must reap the rewards of their perseverance. My advice to you is to get a financial GPS done. Establish your financial goals, and follow the "How Money Works" principals that I shared with you, and you are on your way to building a solid financial foundation for you and your family.

Lynette Barbieri - Entrepreneur, financial expert, strategic connector and sales leader.

Lynette has been running her financial business for 25 years. She is the co-founder of ETTWOMEN and the ETTWomen Foundation. ETTWOMEN exists to support women entrepreneurs and become successful business owners.

She is also BELLA Magazines the Business Development Director Director and BELLA BOSS Editor. She has a reputation for being a connector and a sales "shark." Her knack for adapting her skills across these two industries has played a major role in her success.

Lynette Barbieri

Business Development Director

BELLA Magazine

I would like to thank all the women who have supported me throughout my journey and always having my back you know who you are, my work wife, Vanessa Coppes, for helping me be me and always encouraging me to do more, and to my husband and family for always supporting me, and my mom, I'll love you forever.

MARISSA F. COHEN
- PUBLISHING -

SHARE YOUR STORY.
YOUR VOICE IS IMPORTANT

★ ★ ★ ★ ★

OVER 100 STORIES TOLD, WITH
100% BEST SELLER SUCCESS
RATE

PUBLISHWITHMARISSA.COM

Made in United States
North Haven, CT
08 July 2024